Contents

Acknowledgments **vii**
About the Author **viii**
Introduction **ix**

1 **Get to Know Your Home** 1
Homeowner's Orientation 1
Warranty Coverage 3

2 **Prepare for Routine and Emergency Situations** 9
Documents 9
Emergency Contacts and Procedures 11
Emergency Equipment and Safety Devices 11
Know When to Call in the Pros 11
Schedule for Routine Maintenance 14
Budget for Routine Maintenance 14
Budget for Major Repairs 14
Budget for the Unexpected 17

3 **Understand the Systems in Your Home** 21
The Structural System 21
The Electrical System 24
The Plumbing System 24
The Heating, Ventilation, and Air-Conditioning System . 26
Your Lifestyle 26

4 **Caring for Your Home** 29
Air Conditioning Systems 29
Appliances 33

Attics and Attic Crawl Spaces 34
Bath and Kitchen Ventilation 36
Bathtubs, Lavatories, and Showers 37
Carbon Monoxide Detectors 40
Carpeting 41
Ceiling Fans 42
Chimneys, Fireplaces, and Wood-Burning Appliances 42
Circuit Breakers and Your Home's Electrical System 45
Cleaning Exterior and Interior Surfaces 48
Decks and Platforms 52
Doors 53
Filters 55
Fire Extinguishers 57
Flooring 58
Foundations, Crawl Spaces, and Basements 61
Gutters and Downspouts 64
Heating Systems 65
Home Automation 70
Home Security 74
Landscaping and Yard Care 75
Lead in Paint, Water, and Soil 79
Masonry 81
Painting 82
Paved Surfaces 90
Plumbing 95
Roofs 99
Safety 107
Siding 110
Smoke Detectors 110
Termites and Other Insect Pests 112
Trees and Shrubs 114
Walls 117
Water Heaters 119
Weatherstripping 121
Windows 123

5 A Seasonal Checklist for Maintaining Your Home 127
Air Conditioning Systems 128
Appliances 128
Attics and Attic Crawl Spaces 129
Basements 129
Bathtubs, Showers and Lavatories 129
Carbon Monoxide Detectors 129
Carpeting 130
Ceiling Fans 130
Chimneys and Fireplaces 130
Circuit Breakers and Electrical System 130
Cleaning 131
Crawl Spaces 131
Decks and Platforms 131

Doors **131**
Drains **132**
Driveways, Walkways, Concrete Steps **132**
Faucets, Exterior **132**
Fire Extinguishers **132**
Flooring **132**
Foundations **133**
Furnaces and Heating Systems **133**
Garden **134**
Gutters and Downspouts **134**
Lawns **134**
Paint, Exterior **135**
Paint, Interior **135**
Plumbing **135**
Roofs **136**
Safety and Security **136**
Siding **136**
Septic System **137**
Smoke Detectors **137**
Termite, Insect Treatments **137**
Tools **137**
Trees and Shrubs **138**
Vent Pipe and Roof Jack **138**
Walls and Ceilings, Interior **138**
Water Heater **138**
Windows **139**
Quick Lists **139**

6 The Homeowner's Toolkit **141**
Tools and Supplies **141**
Renting Equipment **148**

Additional Books for Consumers **149**

Figures

Figure 1 How long things last **15**

Figure 2 The six most popular roof styles used in residential construction . . . **23**

Figure 3 Various home automation modules connected to the power lines
in the home are used to control appliances **25**

Figure 4 Desirable flow of air through an average home in warm weather . . . **27**

Figure 5 Example of oil ports indicating the need to manually fill
oil reservoirs **30**

Figure 6 Window air conditioners should be covered for the winter
to prolong service life **32**

Figure 7 Various intake and exhaust vents used in residential
ventilation systems **35**

Figure 8   Example of a free-standing wood-burning stove **43**

Figure 9   Left: An example of a pellet-fired appliance and its components.
Right: An auger inside a pellet-fired appliance automatically
stokes the fire **44**

Figure 10 A typical breaker box has individual switches controlling
each circuit **46**

Figure 11 A typical electrostatic filter arrangement and placement **56**

Figure 12 A typical oil-fired furnace **66**

Figure 13 In an emergency the flow of natural gas to the home can be
stopped by adjusting the cut-off valve **67**

Figure 14 The typical loop formed by the supply of warm air and return
of cool air in a forced-air system **69**

Figure 15 Safety and security devices controlled by home automation
systems are hard-wired to the home's power lines **72**

Figure 16 Example of a home divided into various temperature zones **73**

Figure 17 Making the most of phone line capabilities, a controller can
distinguish between fax, voice, or data calls **75**

Figure 18 A stone retaining wall in need of re-pointing to stabilize the
mortar joints **82**

Figure 19 A traditional snow shovel, an ergonomically designed snow
shovel, and a deep-faced coal shovel offer homeowners a
choice in snow-removal equipment **91**

Figure 20 Water flow to the entire house can be controlled with the
intake valve **97**

Figure 21 Commonly used residential roofing materials **101**

Figure 22 An example of damaged asphalt shingles **106**

Figure 23 The source of the water damage to this wall was not the window
but a roof leak **107**

Figure 24 Close-up view of a termite and the sheltering tubes they travel
through when crossing exposed areas **113**

Figure 25 A common electric water heater showing the exterior components
and water flow into and out of the tank **120**

Figure 26 Weather breaks built into a storm window prevent temperature
transference **124**

Figure 27 An assortment of frequently used painting tools **144**

Figure 28 Typical ladders and scaffolding used when painting **146**

Figure 29 Left: A typical heavy-duty four-cycle snow blower.
Right: A typical medium-duty two-cycle snow blower **148**

Acknowledgments

The author and BuilderBooks extend our thanks to the individuals who reviewed the outline and/or manuscript drafts for this book, and to those who provided comments or information that helped us improve the book:

Lynn Anderson, President, L'Interiors, Fraser, Colorado; Bob Blayden, President, Blayden Design-Build, Renton, Washington; Charlie and Debra Colpo, Glen Allen, Virginia; Daniel Levitan, President, Levitan and Associates, Fort Lauderdale, Florida; David Ellis, Northeast Florida Builders Association, Jacksonville, Florida; David Hollies, President, Home Connections, Inc., Silver Spring, Maryland; Zoe Lagassa, NAHB staff; Charles and Jan Layne, Glen Allen, Virginia; Curtis Ostrom, C.N. Ostrom and Son, Inc., Wayzata, Minnesota; Carol Smith, Home Address, Monument Colorado; and William Young, NAHB staff.

Several of the tips, definitions of terms, and illustrations in this book first appeared in other BuilderBooks publications. With thanks, we have adapted material from *Customer Service for Builders and Remodelers, Building Your Home: An Insider's Guide,* and the *Homeowner Manual Model for Builders,* all by Carol Smith; *Remodeling Your Home: An Insider's Guide* by Carol Davitt; and *Your New Home and How to Take Care of It.* Additional sources were *Housing Facts, Figures, and Trends,* published by the NAHB Economics Department; and the following issues of the NAHB Monthly

Column Service, published by the NAHB Public Affairs Department: No. 35, May 6, 1992; no. 40, October 7, 1992; no. 41, November 4, 1992; no. 45, March 3, 1993; no. 46, March 31, 1993; no. 47, May 5, 1993; no 50, August 4, 1993; no. 53, November 3, 1993; no. 61, July 6, 1994; no. 99, and August 1997. Thanks also to the North Carolina Cooperative Extension Service, North Carolina State University, for online reference information used in fact checking for chapters 4 and 5.

About the Author

James Gerhart has been affiliated with various sectors of the building industry for more than 20 years. His background includes sales and marketing, installation, training, customer relations, and project management while working for building materials manufacturers and distributors as well as with builders and contractors. An industry writer for almost a decade, Mr. Gerhart has authored a variety of magazine articles and how-to pamphlets as well as numerous books.

Introduction

New homeowners work and save and plan for the opportunity to make the single largest investment most people ever make—a home. They are in the unique position of personally enjoying the benefits of their new investment while protecting that investment and even nurturing its growth. The best way to accomplish all three goals is by committing to a schedule of regular maintenance.

Looking after all the routine inspections, repairs, cleaning, and servicing a house requires can be an unwieldy prospect to a new homeowner, and can quickly become overwhelming when something is out of whack and fixing it involves on-the-job-training. The systematic approach to preventive maintenance and repair presented in this book provides homeowners with the basic advice they need to plan ahead, reducing the likelihood that they will be hit by surprise repair bills.

Many well-written guides already exist that provide technical advice and step-by-step instructions for specific do-it-yourself home repair and maintenance tasks. Rather than replicate the highly detailed information in these perfectly good sources, this book highlights critical maintenance tasks that will help you preserve the value of your property.

Chapters 1 through 3 provide an overview of the systems and parts of your home and present an approach to scheduling and budgeting for routine maintenance as well as emergencies.

Chapter 4 details routine care and troubleshooting for most of the major parts of your home, from the grading in your yard to the aerator in your kitchen sink (you'll find it under Plumbing). Chapter 5 organizes home maintenance into a sensible reference list of tasks spread across the seasons. Chapter 6 recommends tools every homeowner should assemble in a basic toolkit, suggests additional tools and materials to acquire as needed, and provides tips for using and storing some of the listed items.

A 150-page book is not large enough to present detailed information on all types of construction and innovative products and materials. We chose instead to focus the book on typical materials and components found in a large number of homes today. For example, many new homes are constructed with asphalt shingle roofs, while relatively few homes have metal roofs. Accordingly, the information on roofing includes more detail on the structure, function, and maintenance of asphalt roofing than it does on metal roofs. Similarly, we have organized the book with a generally representative climate in mind rather than try to cover all variations in climate. While readers in the South will be less interested in parts of the book that describe snow removal (and readers in desert areas may be less concerned with moisture-related maintenance issues) almost all homeowners should be able to find some common ground in this book.

By following the simple maintenance procedures described in these chapters you will reduce repair expenses, increase your comfort, and maintain the investment you have made in your home.

Get to Know Your Home

To help protect your investment and ensure long-lasting satisfaction from your new home, the best thing you can do is become as familiar as possible with all aspects of the house.

Chances are you started to become familiar with your new home even before you decided what house to buy or build. You may have studied floor plans and photographs; toured model homes; and selected carpets, wall coverings, paint colors and fixtures, all the while building a mental image of your ideal home. Still, to help protect your investment and ensure long-lasting satisfaction from your new home, the best thing you can do is become as familiar as possible with all aspects of the house.

Homeowner's Orientation

As your closing date approaches your builder or builder's representative will likely contact you to set up an appointment for a final walk through the property as part of your homeowner's orientation. This tour of the almost-finished home allows you to look over the property and verify that the house includes all of the elements specified in the sales contract. Buyers and builders each benefit from a well-conducted homeowner orientation because any minor problems or miscommunications that may be discovered during the tour and orientation usually can be resolved to both parties' satisfaction before the owner or owners move in.

During a homeowner orientation the builder (or builder's representative) methodically discusses the materials and construction of each part of the house and provides basic information about the location and operation of major systems or features, including:

- furnace and air conditioning systems
- fireplaces
- utility lines, meters, and shutoff valves
- circuit breakers
- home automation systems, if included
- major appliances

The builder will answer your questions and can document any tasks yet to be completed, agreed-upon changes, or other items that require attention. The builder may ask you to sign or initial a *punch list* detailing any additional work to be completed before closing.

Prepare for Your Orientation

A lot of time passes between the contract signing and the homeowner orientation. During that time, you will have made decisions that affected virtually every phase of your new home's construction. Keeping track of the decisions you made and the paperwork related to the building of your house by collecting them in a file, box, or accordion folder will help ensure the pertinent information is handy to refresh your memory as closing day draws near.

Before the orientation meeting ask your builder to provide a copy of the forms or other documentation that will be used at the meeting. Review the contents of your file, read through the orientation forms, and jot down any questions that come to mind. Don't forget to add in questions from other family members—including children—who will also be living in the house. Bring your written questions to the orientation meeting so you don't forget to ask for important information.

The orientation meeting is an important step, not something that should be rushed. Remember: you and the builder ultimately want the same result: customer satisfaction with the house. Now is the time to ask any and all remaining questions about the project. The only "dumb" question is the one that goes unasked.

If you are buying a previously owned home, make a thorough orientation part of your shopping strategy. Prepare a detailed list of questions ahead of time and bring it with you when you tour homes with the selling agent or owner. If you are a serious prospect, agents and owners will do their best to provide you with useful information about the systems, products, and features of the house.

Let an Expert Be Your Guide

During the pre-closing tour consider the builder, builder's representative, or real estate agent the expert guide to your new home. No one else can answer your questions as thoroughly as the builder or agent. Make notes recording every area and feature pointed out by the builder or agent. If the information is not automatically provided, note the locations of plumbing stacks or electrical circuits that are (or will be) hidden behind drywall. Some builders provide diagrams or still photos showing these locations. Others may allow photos to be taken during the pre-closing tour, provided the photography does not disturb the work of tradespeople completing tasks on the site.

Your orientation tour and meeting will follow an agenda that your builder or agent has developed based on his or her experience, feedback from other customers, and the type and complexity of the home. In *Building Your Home: An Insider's Guide,* customer-service expert Carol Smith notes that some companies have lists of as many as 180 items to talk about during new home orientations. "Though you may desperately want to discuss the flat spot in the backyard," she advises, "listen to the steps for cleaning the range hood filter and hold your grading question until the tour goes outside." Go with the flow, using your notes to remind you of important questions so you can devote your attention to what the builder or agent is saying.

Don't be surprised to find that some work still needs to be done. For the most part, the builder will point out such necessary work (or areas that do not meet his or her standards) before you even see them. Room-by-room as needed, check the work on the house against the contract, selection sheets, and any change orders that may exist. Do carpets, paints, tiles, and other details correspond to the materials called for in the paperwork? These items may already be on the punch list. If they aren't, don't be afraid to discuss them with your builder.

Your homeowner orientation may also include a review of the *builder's warranty,* procedures you should follow for requesting work during the warranty period, and *manufacturers' warranties* for appliances such as the dishwasher, washer, dryer, garbage disposal, furnace, and air conditioners. Some builders provide written warranty and service contact information as part of the orientation; others provide partial documentation at the orientation and follow up with the balance of the documentation at closing.

Warranty Coverage

New home buyers have an initial maintenance edge over most buyers of previously owned homes in that the structure, materials, workmanship, and products in new homes are likely to be covered to a greater extent by various warranties.

Even when builders and tradespeople have taken the greatest care to produce an excellent product, defects and problems may arise after you have moved into a new home. Following some simple rules of thumb can save you time and reduce misunderstandings with your builder should you need to request service under any of the warranties that may cover materials or workmanship in your home.

Before you move in, be sure you understand the builder's policies and procedures for warranty service. If the builder does not automatically review these policies during the orientation meeting, ask that they be reviewed before the closing. Ask questions about any policies or procedures that you do not understand.

Read each warranty document and ask for clarification regarding any items that you find confusing. For each warranty, be sure you understand the following:

- what is covered
- what is excluded
- what you must do, if anything, to initiate coverage
- what you must do, if anything, to maintain coverage during the warranty period
- what kinds of events or actions will void the warranty
- when coverage begins
- when coverage ends
- whether extended or additional coverage is available (and if so, under what terms) and
- what you must do to request warranty service

With most new homes, coverage begins on closing. Be sure you understand what kinds of problems are considered emergencies. Different policies and procedures may apply to emergency and nonemergency service.

Store copies of all warranty documentation in a safe, accessible place. (Some people keep originals in a safe deposit box and keep photocopies in a file at home.)

Should a problem arise, find and review the warranty information that covers that specific problem before you request service. After you have identified the problem, notify the appropriate contact in writing as soon as possible. If you phone in a warranty claim, follow up with a written notice specifying all the details of the claim and noting the date, time, and person you spoke with on the telephone. Many builders provide printed service request forms. If your builder does not provide these forms, send a letter that includes the information necessary to accurately document the problem.

Keep a copy of the written notice in your file. Be patient. Depending on the urgency of your claim, you may need to take a back seat to someone else's problem. Depending on the nature of the service required, the work might involve coordination between one or more manufacturers or trades. Bad weather or extreme temperatures may delay some types of work. While it is frustrating to wait for warranty work to be completed, remember that your ultimate satisfaction rests on the work being done properly.

Types of Warranties (New Homes)

Most builders today provide some sort of express warranty, usually in writing, that states the terms and conditions of coverage the builder provides with regard to the structure and components of the house.

A builder's new home limited warranty may be backed by the builder's own resources (self-insured) or backed by the resources of a separate company (insured). A new home limited warranty will usually provide coverage for one year on materials and workmanship. Systems coverage and structural coverage also may be provided to varying degrees.

Under the terms of their contract with the builder trade contractors typically warrant their workmanship and any materials they provide for one year. You may or may not receive copies of specific trade contractor warranties depending on the system your builder has established for contracting and for handling warranty work.

Your builder will *assign,* or pass through to you, the manufacturers' warranties for various materials and parts, including manufacturers' warranties for major appliances. In some cases the manufacturers' warranties may provide coverage that exceeds the coverage provided under the builder's limited warranty. Access to manufacturers' warranty information on some kinds of consumer products is required by federal law, and your builder may have shared or directed you to some of this information during the building process as part of your selection process.

Appliance warranties vary in duration and coverage. To activate manufacturers' warranties you will generally need to complete and mail a registration card to the manufacturer. Builders usually do not become involved in warranty service required for appliances; instead, the homeowner works directly with the manufacturer. Take note: Failing to follow the manufacturers' guidelines for recommended use and maintenance may void the warranty.

Besides the express warranties you receive from the builder you may be covered to some extent by the implied warranty the law assumes to be inherent in the sale of the home to you by the builder. The law assumes the existence of an implied warranty on the basis that (1) the builder is providing a private residence for the buyer and (2) no builder would intentionally provide a product unfit for habitation. Implied warranties are based on either case precedent or state statute. Usually, a homeowner will have to file a lawsuit in order to have an implied warranty enforced.

Buyers of previously owned homes should ask about any applicable warranties before signing the contract; each situation will be different, depending in part on the age of the home and whether any of the original warranties remain in force.

Emergency Warranty Service

Fortunately, emergency service is rarely needed in new homes. A request for emergency warranty service might be in order in the event of:

- total loss of heat
- total loss of air conditioning, depending on the region and local custom
- total loss of electricity, depending on the cause
- a plumbing leak that requires you to shut off the entire water supply
- total loss of water
- gas leak

Follow your builder's policies when placing a request for emergency warranty service. Doing otherwise may inadvertently delay service. No matter whom you call during an emergency, follow up in writing to your builder. If problems arise later you will want documentation of what you reported, to whom, and when.

Nonemergency Service

Most warranty service requests fall into this category. Upon receiving a warranty request the builder may schedule an inspection appointment with you to evaluate the problem and determine which materials and employees or trade contractors will be required to provide the repair. Depending on the availability of materials and workers, response times to complete the warranty work can range from one day to several weeks.

Some builders ask homeowners to place warranty service requests immediately on noticing a problem. Other builders ask that homeowners keep a list and submit warranty claims at one or more designated checkpoints after move-in. Some builders will send reminders to inform homeowners that their warranty is about to expire. However, remembering the expiration date of your warranty coverage is the homeowner's responsibility; your builder is under no obligation to remind you.

Obligations and Limitations

Ideally your new home warranty will clearly state the obligations of the builder and the homeowner and detail any limitations or exclusions. Typically the builder is obligated to repair, replace, or pay the homeowner the reasonable cost of repairing or replacing any defective items covered by the warranty. The warranty may stipulate that the dollar amount of the builder's total liability is limited to the purchase price of the home. Repairs provided by the builder under the terms of the warranty are performed at no charge to the homeowner. Homeowner obligations may include providing normal maintenance and proper care of the home, meeting the builder's specific notification requirements for warranty service, and providing the builder with access to the home to conduct inspections or repair work.

Items excluded from warranty coverage may include the following:

- consequential or incidental damages (depending on state law)
- damage caused by lack of proper maintenance or by the homeowner's failure to take actions to minimize damage and give notice of the defect
- defects caused by the normal wear and tear of living in the home
- acts of God, including major storms, floods, or earthquakes
- damage caused by changes in the grading or drainage patterns surrounding the home's foundation

- damage caused by excessive watering of lawns or plants near the home's foundation
- insect or animal damage

In some situations the cost of repair work not covered by the builder's warranty may be covered by your homeowner's insurance policy or under a guarantee provided by a service contractor (such as a pest control company).

Most builders will temper a literal interpretation of warranty standards with common sense. Nevertheless, the terms and service you can expect usually reflect what has been put in writing. To prevent misunderstandings be sure to study the builder's limited warranty as well as any documented warranty standards and information detailing your own maintenance responsibilities before signing the contract and again before moving into your new home.

Few material things combine science, technology, art, and sweat in quite the same way as a home. With informed expectations you can enjoy the process of caring for your home *and* love the results. Your home is a major investment. It also can become an expression of your personality, a source of pride, and a haven from the bustling modern world.

2

Prepare for Routine and Emergency Situations

Whether you have recently purchased a new or previously owned home or lived in your home for years, you can take the same basic steps to improve your readiness for routine and emergency situations:

- Assemble and read pertinent documents.
- Post emergency contact names and numbers near telephones.
- Know where utility shutoff valves are located, and how to use them.
- Stock your home with basic tools and emergency items.
- Plan and rehearse emergency evacuation procedures.
- Establish a schedule for routine safety and maintenance checks.
- Build funding for short-term and long-term maintenance and repair tasks into your household budget.

Handling both routine and emergency maintenance tasks will be much easier if you have established a well-organized file or notebook containing your home's sales, orientation, warranty, and closing documents.

Documents

As the information in chapter 1 implies, handling both routine and emergency maintenance tasks will be much easier if you have established a well-organized file or notebook containing your home's sales, orientation, warranty, and closing documents. Some homeowners find it easier to keep such materials organized in a large D-ring binder with protective plastic sleeves. (Legal-sized documents can be folded to fit in a letter-sized sleeve for safe storage and removed as needed for review.) Using a binder allows you to flip through documents quickly to find the information you need, and the sturdy binder is easily stored on a shelf or in a bookcase. Manufacturers' instructions and manuals for major appliances also are good candidates for the binder.

If you have purchased a home in a historic district, certain types of maintenance, repair, and remodeling work may require approval by a local architectural review committee or board. Similarly, if you purchase a condominium or a home in a community governed by a community or homeowner's association, your maintenance, repair, and remodeling activities may be guided or restricted by association policies. Before embarking on major repair or remodeling projects you may need to submit plans to an association committee or municipal board and abide by specified limitations and restrictions.

Carefully review any architectural guidelines or requirements and homeowners' association bylaws and policies that may apply to your home, and keep copies alongside the other important documents in your house file or binder. That way, the written guidelines and requirements will be available for quick reference when you need to address a maintenance issue.

Finally, as you conduct repair and maintenance chores, consider keeping a log. The log need not be fancy—a small spiral notebook for jotting down notes and a large manila envelope for collecting receipts work nicely, provided you remember to use them. Or use a specific section in your household file or binder. Besides helping you with your budget, well-organized documentation of maintenance and home improvement activities may come in handy should you have your home reappraised or when you prepare to sell (see What Is the Basis of Your Home?).

What Is the Basis of Your Home? To the Internal Revenue Service, your home's *basis* is a dollar value reflecting the investment you have made in the property. The amount includes the value of capital improvements you may have made. Most routine home maintenance tasks and minor home improvements do not count as capital improvements. Major improvements such as putting on a new roof or remodeling a kitchen are considered capital improvements. Minor repairs or redecorating, such as repainting a room in another color or buying new furnishings, are not considered capital improvements. The basis is not a consideration for routine budgeting; however, it does play a role in long-term financial planning. When you sell your home, you will calculate an adjusted basis for the home you sold. The adjusted basis helps determine the tax you may owe on the money you make from the sale. Keeping thorough and accurate records of your home maintenance and improvement efforts—particularly any major home improvements—will help you calculate an accurate adjusted basis when it comes time to sell. The Internal Revenue Service provides free information about basis, taxes, and deductions in Publication 530 (Tax Information for First-Time Homeowners), Publication 551 (Basis of Assets), and Publication 936 (Home Mortgage Interest Deduction).

If your move to your new home was business-related (for example, you relocated in order to accept a job) and your move was greater than 50 miles, you may be able to able to deduct some of your moving expenses when calculating your federal income taxes. While many moving expenses are not deductible, keep records of expenditures for:

- packing goods and personal effects
- transporting goods and personal items to your new home
- storing household goods and personal effects temporarily, if related to the move, and
- traveling expenses (some, though not all, may be deductible).

Emergency Contacts and Procedures

Keep a written list of emergency contacts posted near one or more telephones. You may also want to keep a copy somewhere off the premises (for example, give one to a family member or friend, or keep a copy in your purse, automobile glove compartment, personal file, or office). Don't forget to write your own address and contact number or numbers on the list. This may seem unnecessary, but during a real emergency you may become confused: simply reading from the list can save you valuable moments. Also, should a guest or babysitter need to make an emergency call he or she will have the information handy. A sample emergency list appears on page 12.

Prepare yourself and your loved ones to take prompt action in the event of a household emergency. Make sure all adults living in the house know basic details such as how to operate water and gas shutoff valves. Determine the best exit routes for each room in the event of fire. Hold emergency drills to make sure everyone remembers what to do. Practicing these drills may feel awkward at first, but doing so helps save lives. Again, in a real emergency you will be under considerable stress; you also may be groggy from sleep, or you may be injured. You may not be thinking clearly. Regular practice can help you remember what to do and proceed more calmly should an emergency arise.

Emergency Equipment and Safety Devices

Make use of safety devices such as smoke alarms, carbon monoxide detectors, and fire extinguishers. Test smoke alarms monthly and change batteries once or twice yearly to be sure they are working properly. More information on common safety devices can be found in the individual listings in chapter 4.

Know When to Call in the Pros

Unless you have the proper training, it's better to call a professional when you experience problems with the major systems in your home. Working on these systems yourself may be unsafe and may make the problem worse.

Emergency Contacts

EMERGENCY: Call 911 or: _____

if in area not served by 911)

Police (Nonemergency): _____

Fire (Nonemergency): _____

Security Company:_____

Poison Control Center:_____

Hospital: _____

Primary Physician:_____

Dentist: _____

Veterinarian: _____

Other:_____

Utilities

Electric Company: _____

Oil or Gas Company: _____

Municipal Water: _____

Services

Electrician: _____

Plumber: _____

HVAC:_____

Insurance Company: _____

Neighborhood

Neighborhood Watch: _____

Homeowners' or

Neighborhood Association: _____

Family

Our Address: _____

_____

Our Phone:_____

Work Phone Numbers: _____

Member(s) of Family or Friends to Contact in Emergency:_____

_____

Electrical

Don't ignore problems with your electrical system. If your lights or appliances don't function normally or if you detect a burning smell, take action. Unless you have experience and the proper training, call in a professional electrician at once. Describe the problem as specifically as possible. The electrician may reassure you that it is a minor problem—or he or she may advise you to shut off all power to the house. Because any electrical repairs or upgrades must pass code inspection, it's best to let a professional handle it right from the start.

Plumbing

Most of us are able to follow basic instructions to handle a clogged drain or replace a worn washer in the kitchen faucet. However, attempting major repairs or plumbing installations without proper training can result in unnecessary water damage. Calling in a professional can be less expensive than tackling the job alone. Also, as with electrical work, major plumbing repairs, changes, or additions may require inspection to ensure that the work complies with code requirements.

Natural Gas

Although natural gas has no inherent smell, a very detectable odor is added to the gas by the supplier to help you notice a leak. Any time you smell natural gas in the home, immediately extinguish any open flames, including any smoking materials. Leave the house at once and call your gas utility service to report a leak. They will dispatch a service technician to safely repair the problem and restore service to your home.

If you have a minor problem, such as occasionally having to relight a pilot light, do not turn the gas off at the main. You can regulate the flow of gas by using the shutoff valve located at the appliance. In each case, carefully follow the step-by-step instructions for lighting the pilot in the manufacturer's manual or posted on the appliance itself. If you use a gas stove, regularly check the cleanliness and height of the flame. Clean gas stoves regularly to prevent grease buildup that can interfere with a clean flame. It is generally recommended that homeowners not store any potentially explosive or flammable materials, including cleaning materials, in the vicinity of gas appliances.

Many appliances use electronic pilot ignitions that automatically control the pilot lights. These systems are easy to use and are generally safer than the continuous pilot systems found on older gas appliances.

If the pilot light on a gas appliance frequently goes out, this may be a sign of more serious problems. Call your utility company and/or a professional service company to inspect the appliance. Often a minor adjustment or repair will suffice, but it is best not to let a minor problem escalate to a dangerous one.

Schedule for Routine Maintenance

Basically, there are two ways to prepare yourself for routine home maintenance tasks: (1) build time for them into your schedule and (2) supply yourself with the basic tools and materials you will need. Chapter 5 provides a checklist you can use to develop your own schedule for routine maintenance and chapter 6 provides a startup list of tools and supplies most homeowners find handy for routine tasks. Scheduling and tools both warrant a quick mention in a chapter on preparation, however, simply because many homeowners put them off until trouble strikes. Like many long-term commitments, caring for your home will be much easier, less costly, and more rewarding if you plan ahead and keep the right tools at hand.

You have a lot of flexibility in scheduling most maintenance tasks. Many routine maintenance and repair tasks can be done at any time of year, and assigning a task to a particular month or season is far less important than simply setting a regular date to do it! The seasonal approach taken in this book simply offers one way to schedule routine tasks so that the list does not become overwhelming at any given time.

Budget for Routine Maintenance

The simplest way to budget for routine maintenance is to create a place for it in a written household budget. Include amounts to cover specific tasks according to your projected schedule. Don't forget to include projected costs for routine cleaning and supplies. If you wish, divide the annual amount by 12 to establish a target monthly amount. Assuming you won't use the full amount each month (for maintenance or by diverting it to another expense), the amount will slowly grow so that it easily accommodates the costs of the various tasks that come up during the year.

Your initial maintenance and repair budget will likely be something of a guess. How much you'll need will depend on a number of factors, including whether you've purchased a new or previously owned home, what products, materials, and workmanship are covered under warranty, and whether you wish to make changes or improvements to your home or yard in the coming year. To refine your budget from year to year, refer to your maintenance log— or to the service and store receipts for the costs of services, materials, and supplies you purchased during the last year.

Over time you will gain a realistic sense of the amount you actually spend (or need to spend) each year on home maintenance and repair. You will also begin to see patterns that can help you plan for more efficient use of your maintenance dollars.

Budget for Major Repairs

Buying a home is the single largest personal expense most of us will ever incur. At times it may seem the expense of maintaining that home runs a very close second, but recent figures show owning a home is a real bargain. While annual inflation has recently averaged about 3.5 percent, the costs associated with five key spending categories for the home have averaged an annual increase of just 2 percent. Still, it's important to plan for major repairs.

Many factors go into the specific lifespan of each component of your home. Figure 1 presents some general guidelines for when you might expect major expenses. Keep in mind the durations given in Figure 1 are general guidelines and do not represent a standard for any particular appliance, product, or material.

FIGURE 1 How Long Things Last

Item	Life in Years	Item	Life in Years
Appliances		Interior—solid core	30-lifetime
Compactors	10	Exterior—protected overhang	80-100
Dishwashers	10	Exterior—unprotected and exposed	25-30
Dryers	14	Folding	30-lifetime
Disposal	10	Garage doors	20-50
Freezers	12-16	Garage door opener	10
Microwave ovens	11	**Electrical**	
Ranges—electric	17	Copper wiring	100+
Ranges—gas	19	Insulation	Lifetime
Ranges, high oven—gas	14	**Finishes**	
Refrigerators	14-17	Paint, plaster, stucco	3-5
Washers	13	Sealer, silicone, waxes	1-5
Exhaust fan	20	**Floors**	
Bathrooms		Oak or pine	Lifetime
Cast iron bathtub	50	Slate flagstone	Lifetime
Fiberglass bathtub		Vinyl, sheet or tile	20-30+
and shower	10-15	Terrazzo	Lifetime+
Shower doors (average quality)	25	Carpeting	11
Toilet	50	Marble	Lifetime+
Cabinets		**Footings and Foundations**	
Kitchen cabinets	15-20	Poured footings and Foundations	200
Medicine cabinets, bath vanities	20	Concrete block	100
Ceilings		Cement	50
Ceiling suspension	Lifetime	Waterproofing (bituminous coating)	10
Acoustical ceiling	Lifetime	Termite proofing	5
Closet Systems		Baseboard system	20
Closet shelves	Lifetime	**Gutters, Downspouts**	30
Countertops		**Heating, Ventilation and Air Conditioning**	
Laminate	10-15	Air-conditioning unit	
Ceramic tile (high grade)	Lifetime	Central unit	15
Wood, butcher block	20+	Window unit	10
Granite	20+	Compressor	15
Doors		Humidifier	8
Screen	25-50		
Interior—hollow core	Less than 30 lifetime		*(Continued)*

FIGURE 1 (*Continued*)

Item	Life in Years
Heating, Ventilation and Air Conditioning (*Continued*)	
Water heater	
Electric	14
Gas	11-13
Forced-air furnaces	
Heat pumps	15
Ductwork	
Plastic	15
Galvanized	30
Rooftop air conditioners	15
Boilers, hot water (steam)	30
Furnaces (gas or oil)	18
Unit heaters (gas or electric)	13
Radiant heaters	
Electric	10
Hot water or steam	25
Air terminals	
Diffusers, grilles, registers	27
Induction and fan-coil units	20
Dampers	20
Fans	
Centrifugal	25
Axial	20
Ventilating roof-mounted	20
Coils	
DX, water, or steam	20
Electric	15
Heat exchangers	
Shell-and-tube	24
Molded insulation	20
Pumps (sump and well)	10
Burners	21
Home Security Appliances	
Intrusion systems	14
Smoke detectors	12
Smoke, fire, intrusion systems	10
Insulation	
Foundation, roof, ceiling, wall, floor	Lifetime
Landscaping	
Wooden decks	15
Brick and concrete patios	24
Tennis courts	10
Concrete walks	24
Gravel walks	4
Asphalt driveway	10
Swimming pool	18
Sprinkler systems	12

Item	Life in Years
Fences	12
Masonry	
Chimney, fireplace, brick veneer	Lifetime+
Brick and stone walls	100+
Stucco and mantels	Lifetime
Materials	
Caulking (for sealer)	8-10
Metal (for coping)	20-40
Mortar (for walls) and plastic	
(for flashing)	25+
Millwork	
Stairs	50-100
Rails and disappearing stairs	30-40
Paints and Stains	
Exterior paint on wood, brick,	
aluminum	7-10
Interior paint on walls, trim, and doors	5-10
Plumbing	
Waste pipe	
Concrete	50-100
Cast iron	75-100
Sinks	
Enamel steel	5-10
Enamel cast iron	25-30
China	25-30
Faucets (low quality)	13-15
Faucets (high quality)	15-20
Roofing	
Asphalt and wood	
shingles and shakes	15-30
Tile	50
Slate	50-100
Sheet metal	20-50+
Built-up roofing	
Asphalt	12-25
Coal and tar	12-30
Asphalt composition	
shingle	15-30
Asphalt overlay	25-35
Rough Structure	
Basement floor system	Lifetime
Wall framing	Lifetime
Shutters	
Wood, interior	Lifetime
Vinyl, interior	Lifetime
Aluminum, interior	35-50
Wood, exterior	4-5

Item	Life in Years	Item	Life in Years
Shutters (Continued)		**Walls and Wall Treatments**	
Vinyl, exterior	7-8	Drywall and plaster	30-70
Aluminum, exterior	3-5	Ceramic tile (high-grade installation)	Lifetime
Siding		Wallpaper	7
Wood	10-100	**Windows**	
Metal (steel)	50-lifetime	Window glazing	20
Aluminum	20-50	Wood casement	20-50
Vinyl	50	Aluminum casement	10-20
		Screen	25-50

Source: NAHB Life Expectancy Survey, from Housing Facts, Figures, and Trends, 1997.

Note: The life expectancies listed are based on average materials and installations, unless otherwise noted, and assume regular routine maintenance. The life expectancy of actual products may be shorter or longer than that listed, depending on the finish or grade, the specific material or combination of materials used, the quality of the design and installation, and other factors.

Many people find it convenient to pay for major home repairs and improvement projects using a home equity line of credit or a home equity loan (often called a second mortgage). Paying for anything on credit costs more than paying for it up front, but certain types of loans may carry income tax advantages.

Of course, building equity in your new home takes time. Fortunately, if you have purchased a new home, chances are you will have accumulated considerable equity by the time you face a major repair or replacement cost. If you also have steadily accumulated money in long-term savings, you will have built up a strong asset base against which to borrow the sum necessary for the repair.

When a major repair or replacement job becomes a necessity, request estimates for the work from two or three reputable contractors. Be sure to give exactly the same information and request estimates for the exact same work from all contractors whose bids you plan to compare. If your instructions vary, each contractor's pricing may be based on slightly different assumptions—and you may wind up comparing apples to oranges.

You may be quoted a single bottom-line figure that covers labor, material, transportation, building permits, insurance, and other overhead costs. If you have obtained several estimates and the bottom-line amounts are fairly close, you can be reasonably confident the the contractor you select will be able to complete the work as budgeted. If the bids vary greatly, check your instructions (and the contractors' assumptions). Make sure you and the contractors have the same understanding about the scope of the work to be done, and request new estimates if necessary.

Budget for the Unexpected

Budgeting for unexpected emergencies basically comes down to saving for a rainy day. Saving can seem hard, or even impossible to a homeowner facing

Budgeting Example: Replacing a Roof:
Depending on your roof type, the materials used, its longevity and condition, and the number of years you remain in your home, roof maintenance and repair tasks may range from very minor to complete replacement. Because roof replacement is a costly prospect, it makes a good example for long-term budgeting.

To project the costs for a new roof, you will need to do some fieldwork and perform a few calculations. First, you must measure the roof area to determine the quantity of roofing material needed. Most of the time, these measurements can be done from the ground.

To measure the area of the roof, visually break up the space into easily measured shapes (squares, rectangles, or triangles). Calculate the area of each section then add the numbers together for the total area of the roof.

Because the roofing industry operates with units of measure called *squares*, it is convenient to convert all roofing measurements into squares. Each square equals 100 square feet. If the roof has valleys that need covering, one additional square of roofing is needed for every 100 linear feet of valley. A dormer in the roof adds another square of material to the total. (A simple roof area of 2,000 square feet would be covered by 20 squares of material; if the roof had 200 linear feet of valley and two dormers, the number would go up to 24 squares.)

Talk to the professionals at the local building supply company. Price one or more types of shingles based on warranty, fire resistance, and wind resistance. Remember: a bundle of shingles does not equal one square. Roofing material usually comes four bundles to the square. If your roof requires 24 squares of material you will need to buy at least 96 bundles of shingles, plus some extra material to account for waste.

Keep two things in mind: (1) measure the material according to industry conventions (not all materials are measured in the same way); and (2) always build in a little extra to account for waste materials. Once you have determined the total area of your roof, a good rule of thumb is to add in a waste factor of 10 percent.

Multiply the cost per bundle or per square by the amount of material needed for your roof. Then increase this figure by 25 percent to cover the cost for items such as nails, flashing, and roof cement. This will give you a ballpark figure for material costs.

Be sure to factor labor costs into your budget. Average wages for roofers currently run about $26.25 per hour; apprentices work for about $10.50. The size and complexity of the job will determine the number of workers, but two roofers and one or two apprentices is not unusual. Simple re-roofing can take three days or more while a tear-off and replacement can take up to a week or even longer.

To the basic labor costs, factor in an amount equal to the cost of any necessary building permits plus any anticipated amounts a contractor builds in to cover overhead, insurance, transportation, and other miscellaneous costs.

Professional roofers are much more accurate with measurements and calculations, so don't be surprised if your estimate is different from the professional estimates you receive. Pricing for materials and labor will also reflect other factors. Ask yourself (and your roofer) these questions:

- Does the entire roof need to be replaced or only sections that have been damaged?

(Continued)

Budgeting Example (*Continued*)

- Does the wood or plywood underlayment need to be replaced? If so, is replacement needed everywhere or only for portions of the roof?
- Will the new roof be put on over the existing roof or must the old roof be torn off?
- What type and weight shingle are you selecting for the new roof?

When you request estimates for a roofing job, ask each contractor how the shingles will be delivered and handled on the job-site. Can the contractor have the shingles delivered directly to the roof? Doing this saves labor and time as workers won't need to carry each bundle up a ladder to the roof.

If you have bought a new home with an asphalt shingle roof, your new roof will last for approximately 15 to 30 years. Let's assume for budgeting that you plan on needing to re-roof in 25 years. Setting up a budget for a roof purchase 25 years away requires adjusting the cost estimate for inflation and having discipline. Build in a fudge factor to allow for unforeseen costs. Although it may not match the exact current rate of inflation, 3 percent works well as an estimate for inflation.

If the cost of having the roof re-done is currently $6,000, a year from now the same re-roof would cost $6,180 ($6,000 + 3 percent). If a 3 percent increase was calculated each year for 25 years, the projected cost comes to $12,562.66.

---

an immediate crisis. The trick is to separate long-term from short-term savings goals, and to arrange your budget so that money targeted for long-term goals remains unaffected by variations in your short-term finances.

Financial planners often recommend setting aside enough money in liquid (easily accessible) savings to cover three, six, or even more months' living expenses should you lose your job or face some other crisis that lowers or eliminates your income. One way to approach saving for home emergencies is to simply add another month's expenses to this target figure. If doing this seems hard, consider how much more expensive it will be to pay interest on the same amount if you must put the cost on credit.

Small amounts regularly set aside can grow over time into a comfortable emergency fund—particularly if your savings are earning interest. Specific advice on household budgeting or investing is beyond the scope of this book. Homeowners should consider a broad range of savings options.

Budgeting Checklist: Follow these steps to plan ahead for routine, long-term, and emergency maintenance and repair tasks:

Routine Care
1. Make a list of any anticipated repair or improvement projects you wish to undertake in the coming year (for example, replace gutters, install new window locks, repair wood or concrete steps, build a crushed stone pathway in the garden, and so forth).
2. List the specific tools you expect to buy or replace, based on the listed

(Continued)

Budgeting Checklist (*Continued*)

projects.

3. List the specific materials you will need to complete the listed projects.
4. List any items you will rent in order to complete the listed projects.
5. List the cleaning supplies you regularly use in a general category (Cleaning).
6. List replacement items such as filters for your furnace, air conditioner, or other air-filtering equipment.
7. List items you anticipate needing as "Occasional Supplies" (for example, batteries, lightbulbs).
8. Assign a projected cost to each item or category, based on prices you have observed while shopping and on quantities needed to cover one year.
9. Divide the annual budget by 12 to create a target amount for your monthly budget.
10. Record maintenance activities and expenses in a notebook or log; the log can help you fine-tune your budget over time.

Long-Term Projects

1. Commit to making regular contributions to long-term savings; if possible, dedicate a specific portion of long-term savings to home repair and maintenance.
2. Assess the overall condition of your home. What major repairs or replacements are likely to be needed within the next 5 years? 10 years? 20 years?
3. Create a rough estimate of the cost in materials and labor for each major item you have identified (or obtain estimates from contractors).
4. Factor in cost increases over time and project the amounts you will need to accomplish the work as it becomes necessary.
5. Consider how you can best position yourself to meet these long-term costs using a combination of cash, accumulated savings, and sensible credit.

Emergencies

1. Determine the amount you can maintain in liquid savings as a cushion against general emergencies, including emergency household repairs (for example, 3 or more months' worth of expenses).
2. Divide the amount by 12 to establish a target for monthly savings.
3. Assess this cushion every year; add to it as needed to replace money used or to build the amount over time.
4. Document household appliances, products, and possessions accurately for warranty and insurance purposes. Review and update this information annually or as needed when you acquire new products.
5. Should emergency repairs or replacements be covered by your homeowner's insurance, be sure to reimburse your emergency savings immediately once you receive the insurance payment.

Review all budgets annually.

3

Understand the Systems of Your Home

Thinking of home maintenance in terms of the major systems that need support can help put the many tasks involved into perspective. For purposes of home maintenance, a house can be thought of as having four major systems: a structural system, an electrical system, a plumbing system, and a heating, ventilation, and air-conditioning system.

The Structural System

Think of the structural system as the parts of the house that give it shape and substance—the framing that holds it up, the roof and walls that keep out the weather. While it may not be scientifically exact, we will consider the term *structural* to refer to parts of the house whose physical presence or mechanical function helps support or protect the house. For example, gutters and downspouts obviously are not structural in the same way as framing timbers; however, they are physical structures that direct water down and away from the roof and walls, helping to protect the house from water damage. Similarly, insulation, housewraps, and roofing membranes don't hold parts of the house together; but each acts as a physical barrier to heat and moisture, working as part of a structural system to protect your home from the elements.

Some structural elements are easily seen; others are more subtle, hidden behind finished walls, ceilings, and floors. If

A house can be thought of as having four major systems: a structural system, an electrical system, a plumbing system, and a heating, ventilation, and air-conditioning system.

you follow the definition given above, maintaining the structural system of your home basically comes down to preventing damage to the physical structures that protect and support the home. Such prevention is largely passive: remembering that these structures are in place and avoiding actions that damage the structural system. For example, the layers just underneath roofing shingles can be easily damaged by specific pressure, such as the weight of someone walking on the roof. Damage to these layers can lead to major problems with moisture penetration and leaks that can be hard to pinpoint—a potentially expensive hassle. The other aspect of structural maintenance is to be prompt about repairing damage when it occurs. Procrastination can lead to serious and expensive problems.

Structural Design

Your home is much more than a fashionable box. Your home's structural design addresses issues related to weight and stress: holding up floors and walls; evenly distributing the weight of the house on well-prepared soil so the structure remains stable and does not sink or slide; ensuring that walls won't collapse under heavy winds; and so forth. If you make major changes to a house, such as adding rooms or knocking down walls to expand interior space, take care to maintain the structural integrity of the house so that none of these functions is undermined.

Of course, architects and designers solve engineering problems in a wide variety of ways—most homes are not just boxes. Roofs again provide a good example of how structural designs can vary while basically performing the same function.

Types of Roofs

Most roofing is divided into two types: low slope and steep slope. Slope is a measure of elevation. Roofs with a very low slope (as little as 1/8 inch per foot) often are referred to as flat roofs. However, because a truly flat roof would collect water, or pond, when it rains all roofs have at least a slight slope. On residential structures low-slope roofs are mainly found on porches, extensions, carports, and garages. Steep-slope roofs have slopes of varying angles, some greater than 2 1/2 inches per foot, which help the roof shed water.

The most popular styles of roofs used in residential construction are the *gable, hip, shed, gambrel,* and *mansard* styles (Figure 2). Complex designs for larger houses may use variants and even combinations of these basic styles.

Gable roofs are named for the triangular section of end wall between the rafter plate (the top of the wall on which the ends of the roof rafters are seated) and the roof *ridge.* The ridge is the high point at or near the center of the house that extends from one end wall to the other. The roof slopes downward from the ridge on either side, ending at the eaves.

In traditional gable roofs the size and slope of the roof on one side of the ridge equals the size and slope of the roof on the other side.

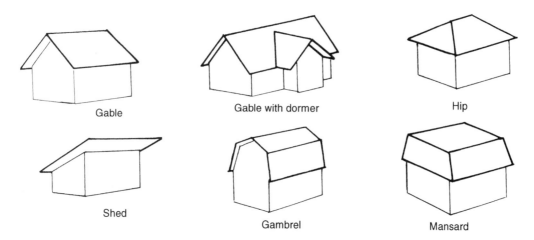

Gable   Gable with dormer   Hip

Shed   Gambrel   Mansard

FIGURE 2 The six most popular roof styles used in residential construction.

Hip roofs also have a ridge but they do not have gable ends. The four sections of the roof slope downward to the eaves on all four sides. Thus the eave edges are at a constant height. The point where two roof surfaces meet at an outside corner is called a *hip*; the junction where two roof surfaces meet at an inside corner is called a *valley*.

Shed roofs slope in only one direction. One side of the house is taller than the other. A variation of the shed roof, the *butterfly roof*, comprises two shed roofs sloped toward a low point at the middle of the house. Two shed roofs sloped upward from the eaves but not meeting at a ridge form yet another variation. The wall separating the two roofs is called a clerestory and often contains windows that add natural light to the interior of the structure.

The *gambrel roof* (or *barn roof*) can be identified by its double slopes—one pair of gentle slopes and one pair of steep slopes. Like a gable roof, the gambrel has a center ridge from which the roof slopes in two directions. At a point about halfway between the ridge and the eave edge, the slope becomes much steeper. Homes with gambrel roofs often have attic rooms with dormers that project through the roof for light and ventilation.

The *mansard roof* resembles the hip roof in that it drops from a shorter ridge line in two distinct slopes to eaves of equal height all the way around the house. With this distinctive style of roof, a building can be designed to display up to 40 percent of the outside structure as roof. Mansard roofs are popular for homes, apartment complexes, commercial buildings, and schools.

For most homeowners, the materials, features, and maintenance issues associated with the electrical, plumbing, and HVAC systems are more familiar. We use these systems nearly every day and the components of these systems require regular cleaning, inspection, and "tune-ups." Components of these systems may need repair or replacement more frequently than do structural components, but the repair or replacement is generally less costly. (Consider the relative cost of replacing a hot water tank versus a roof.)

The Electrical System

The electricity you use at home comes in from the electric company via overhead or underground wires and through a service entrance to a meter that tracks your household's consumption. The utilities service entrance often is located along the side of the house or in a basement, garage, or crawl space. To help you execute necessary repairs and prevent unnecessary damage, become familiar with the location and operation of the control mechanisms for all major utilities and systems in your home.

When it leaves the meter, the electricity continues on to a *service panel* that breaks it down into a series of *circuits*. These circuits deliver electrical current throughout the house. *Circuit breakers* in the service panel control individual circuits and protect against fire, which could develop if a circuit draws more current than it's designed to handle. (Information about checking and maintaining circuit breakers appears in chapter 4.)

Electrical current flows under pressure through the wiring in your house. That flow would come to a halt if you were to disconnect every appliance, light, and device in the home. As soon as a device becomes active again, the flow of current resumes in that particular circuit.

The amount of the current flowing through a circuit at any given time is measured in *amperes,* or *amps,* based on the number of electrons passing a certain point each second. The pressure that forces the electrons along their route is called *voltage* and is measured in *volts*.

Increasing the voltage does not accelerate the flow of current because current travels at a constant speed (the speed of light). What does increase is the power in your lines. That power is measured in *watts*. Watts are equal to amps times volts. Your utility bills are based on the number of watts (in thousands) you consume each hour; that's where the term *kilowatt-hour* comes from.

As noted in chapter 2, most new homeowners wisely leave checking, adjusting, and repairing electrical circuitry to the pros. But homeowners can unwittingly set themselves up for problems if they use extension cords improperly, overload circuits by plugging in appliances that, when combined, draw too many amps, or inadvertently damage wiring or connections. Understanding the way the circuits are set up in your home will help you use the system wisely and recognize minor problems before they become major.

Many homes today also include specialized wiring for computerized functions. Such *home automation* features may include automated lighting, security features, home theater systems, computer-controlled thermostats, and other features (Figure 3). Familiarity with your home's circuitry, the capacity of your electrical service, and your options for expanding the service will be helpful should you plan to add or upgrade home automation features.

The Plumbing System

In most homes, the plumbing system comprises two major elements: the *supply lines* and the *drainage, waste, and vent (DWV) lines,* which act independently of

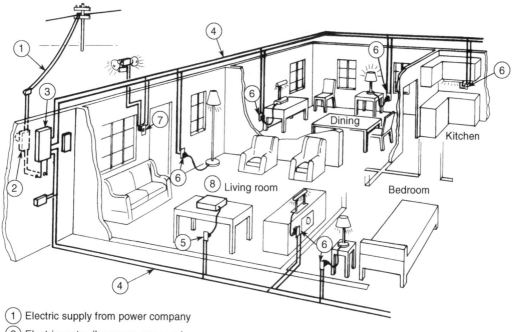

1. Electric supply from power company
2. Electric meter (by power company)
3. Circuit breaker box/panel
4. Standard household wiring circuit
5. Standard electrical outlet and wiring
6. X-10 unit at outlet
7. X-10 unit at wall switch
8. Control unit

FIGURE 3 Various home automation modules connected to the power lines in the home are used to control appliances.

one another. Because most of your home's plumbing components are hidden behind or beneath finish materials (walls, floors, and ceilings), about all you see are the fixtures and an occasional pipe disappearing into a wall or floor.

Supply Lines

A sizable pipe carries water into your house from a municipal water line or from a private well. If you are connected to a municipal water supply, the water will flow through a meter that monitors your usage. At some point after leaving the meter, the supply line splits. One branch feeds into the water heater before continuing on to various hot water fixtures. If you have a private system, the water may collect in a pressure tank before going to the water heater. In some houses, water may be routed through a filtration or treatment system before entering the hot water heater. The second line services cold water needs throughout the house. Like the hot water line, it splits into smaller pipes that go to individual fixtures.

DWV Lines

The DWV portion of your plumbing system depends on gravity to rid the house of liquid and solid wastes. These lines also serve as a passageway to the outside for foul and potentially harmful gases.

The fixtures may drain into the main drain, or *stack,* or into horizontal lengths of pipe that slope toward the stack. Horizontal pipes more than a few feet long must be vented in compliance with local codes, usually via a short vertical run and a *circuit vent* that returns to the stack. These pipes generally run within normal-thickness walls and floors.

Heating, Ventilation, and Air Conditioning System

Air enters and leaves a house in three ways. By *infiltration,* air flows through construction joints and cracks around the windows, doors, foundation, or from crawl spaces underneath a house. *Natural ventilation* occurs when air enters through opened windows and doors. *Mechanical ventilation* devices range from outdoor-vented fans that remove air from a single room to air-handling systems that mix outdoor and indoor air for the entire house. Given today's tightly built homes, keeping the ventilation system in your home operating properly is more important than ever before.

Well-ventilated houses are not only more comfortable in both winter and summer, they're relatively free of many pollutants that can cause health problems. Many homes require more than just incidental ventilation. Symptoms of inadequate ventilation include:

- condensation on the inner surface of windows and on metal surfaces such as hinges and handles (Condensation on storm windows usually indicates a leaky window, not a tight house.)
- stuffy air or lingering odors
- odors from incomplete furnace combustion, back puffing, smoke, or poor draft in the furnace chimney
- back drafts and smoking fireplaces
- slight nausea, constant headaches, or chronic eye or respiratory irritation

A desirable air flow pulls air through the house and supports a controlled, regular exchange of inside and outside air. As seen in Figure 4, a number of components of the heating, ventilation, and air conditioning system work together to maintain air flow: the blower in the heating or air conditioning unit; ducts to carry warmed or cooled air; soffit vents, which allow fresh air in; registers, and vents.

Your Lifestyle

While not technically a system of your home, your lifestyle has a great effect on your home's interior environment and your maintenance priorities. Factors that can influence your approach to caring for your home include:

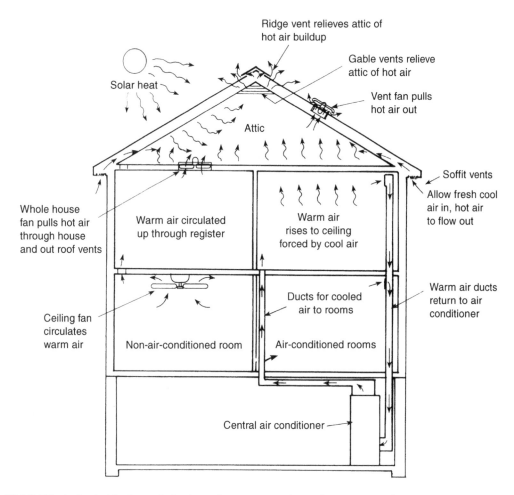

FIGURE 4 Desirable flow of air through an average home in warm weather.

- the number, ages, and habits of the people in your household (traffic patterns, hobbies, personal habits such as smoking, and so forth)
- the number and types of your pets (sources of allergens, cleaning considerations)
- your furnishings (materials, ease of cleaning, potential off-gassing)
- your preferred cooking styles (moisture levels in the kitchen)
- your housekeeping and maintenance habits
- your preferred style and frequency of entertaining

While the influence of each lifestyle choice may be subtle—a short-cold-shower taker generates less moisture and humidity in the bathroom than a long-hot-bath taker—your specific needs and preferences (along with those of the rest of your household) have a cumulative effect on your home, including how much wear and tear you put on specific systems, products, or materials.

Prescribing an optimum lifestyle for easy home maintenance would be an impossible task—too many variables are involved. And the point, after all, is not to treat your home as a fragile museum piece, but to live well in it. However, becoming aware of the ways your use of the home affects various maintenance needs will help keep you in the driver's seat as you enjoy your home for many years to come.

Chapters 1 through 3 have presented information designed to acquaint you with your home's major systems, so that you can approach specific maintenance or repair tasks with an understanding of their context. The next chapter presents specific tips on caring for your home from air conditioners and attic fans to windows and wood-burning appliances.

4

Caring for
Your Home

For easy reference this chapter is organized in alphabetized sections. Some sections are larger and more detailed than others, depending on the complexity of the maintenance tasks involved. Cross references are provided to help you find related material and topics listed under more general headings. To find specific material quickly, look at the running heads atop the pages; each coordinates with the major topic or topics on that page.

To find specific material quickly, look at the running heads atop the pages; each coordinates with the major topic or topics on that page.

Air Conditioning Systems

A properly maintained air conditioning system will give you years of reliable service. Central air conditioning typically incorporates the same temperature controls, ductwork, vents, registers, and grilles as the home's primary heating system (see Heating Systems). Window air conditioning units come in a variety of styles that are rated according to their cooling power and the amount of power required to operate them. Important components of your home's cooling and air circulation system include the compressor, circulating pump, and air filters.

Routine Care

Each spring, check the area around the outdoor unit (the compressor) to make sure it is not blocked by debris, leaves, lawn furniture, or toys. Prune trees and shrubs so that they are no closer than 18 inches from the compressor to ensure adequate airflow. Keep a central air compressor or window air conditioner clear of lawnmower cuttings. Clean air exchangers and clean or change filters on window units every two months during the cooling season.

Each spring check the lines and connections to and from the compressor for crimps or splitting as well as any signs of damage from winter storms. If you notice any significant damage, have the unit checked out by a service technician before using the system.

Lubrication

Most heating and air-conditioning systems have sealed, self-lubricating compressors and circulating motors. However, if you see oiling ports you will need to manually lubricate the system from time to time, following the manufacturer's instructions (see Figure 5). The ports may be difficult to see or reach. They may be on a slant or straight up, or even buried deep within the unit.

Check the oil level at the beginning of each season. As necessary, fill to the top using 10W30 or 10W40 motor oil. Heavier oils will tend to clog and gum up the bearings; lighter oils can't hold up against the heat, lose their viscosity, and dissipate too quickly.

Blower Compartment

Turn off all power to the unit, open the blower compartment, and look over its components. Gently scrape the accumulated dust and grime off the blades,

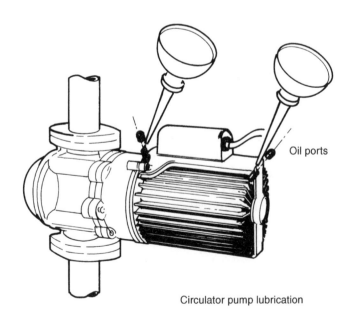

Oil ports

Circulator pump lubrication

FIGURE 5 Example of oil ports indicating the need to manually fill oil reservoirs.

then remove the residue with a vacuum. Wipe the surface clean with a dry, clean cloth. If you notice frayed wires or charred wire insulation, contact a service technician right away.

Professional Cleaning and Inspection

Consult your instruction manual about how often to schedule a professional inspection and cleaning; annual or semiannual inspections are typical recommendations.

Tips for Efficient Operation

You can save power and reduce stress on the unit if you:

- keep doors and windows shut while units are on
- keep draperies and blinds closed on windows that receive direct sunlight
- close registers in rooms not in use
- operate heat-generating appliances, such as ovens, dryers, or dishwashers, during cooler morning or evening hours
- set your thermostat higher at night

If possible, take advantage of landscaping to shade the east and west sides of your house. Keep vents and registers clean and regularly clean or change air filters to maintain good air quality and protect the system's motor against damage from accumulated dirt (see also Filters; Bath and Kitchen Ventilation; and ventilation information in chapter 3).

Troubleshooting

If your air conditioner is not cooling properly, check the following items before calling a repair service:

- Has the thermostat been accidentally reset?
- Are the supply registers in each room fully open?
- How long have the air filters gone unchanged?
- Is airflow blocked around the compressor unit, air outlets, or return registers?
- Are the compressor's fan blades laden with noticeable dirt or grime?
- What is the condition of the ductwork?
- Does uninsulated ductwork run through hot areas (such as unfinished attics or crawl spaces)?
- Is the system making unusual sounds?

A loud squeaking sound may mean that a component needs lubrication or a fan belt is slipping. If a loud rattling noise accompanies the squeaking sound and your circulating pump has oiling ports, add oil and rerun the system. If the squeaking does not stop after several minutes, call the service technician. Thumping sounds can indicate a broken or loose belt or a piece of sheet metal that is expanding and contracting, in which case it is best to have a trained service technician investigate and handle the repairs.

The cost to replace a central air-conditioning system will vary depending on a number of factors, including the cooling requirements of your home. Even a small central unit currently runs around $1,000 installed. Plan on a lifespan of approximately 15 years for a central air-conditioning system and 10 years for window units.

Emergencies

A total loss of air conditioning may be considered an emergency condition, depending on the area of the country in which you live. If you are a senior citizen or have a serious medical condition for which prolonged loss of service could result in a medical emergency, be sure to advise your power company or service technician of this fact when you call for help.

Window Air Conditioners

After the cooling season is over remove window air conditioners and place them in a dry storage area. If circumstances prohibit removal, cover the outside part of the unit using an insulated air-conditioner jacket (Figure 6). These specialty jackets prevent air infiltration through the air conditioner into the home and protect the internal workings of the unit. Such jackets also are available for compressors, protecting the unit from debris, snow, and ice.

▶ **Air-Filtering Systems—See Filters**

▶ **Aluminum Siding—See Siding**

Window unit cover

Outside unit cover

FIGURE 6 Window air conditioners should be covered for the winter to prolong service life. Covers also are available for the outside units of central air-conditioning systems.

Appliances

Your home probably came with one or more of the following electric or gas-powered appliances:

- conventional range or oven
- garbage disposal
- microwave oven
- refrigerator or freezer
- washer and dryer

Routine Care

The instruction manuals you received for these appliances will include details about any required maintenance service, including the manufacturer's recommendations for cleaning and service frequency. In some cases, specific utensils may need to be used or avoided to prevent damage to the appliance (for example, no metal in microwaves, no glass or copper-bottomed cookware on some flat cooking surfaces). Read the instructions carefully and be sure to mail in any documents necessary to record warranties. Record contact information for authorized or recommended service dealers in your address book.

Most electric appliances need little routine care other than regular cleaning. Routine safety precautions include correct handling of electrical cords, proper insertion and removal of plugs, and using outlets carrying the correct amount of power.

Besides regular cleaning, gas appliances such as ranges, dryers, and heating units may need periodic adjustment by a service technician to ensure that the flame burns cleanly and at an appropriate height. A dirty flame reduces the efficiency of the appliance and produces higher levels of dangerous gases such as carbon monoxide.

Clean the gaskets and condenser coils of refrigerators and standalone freezers every three months or so to keep the condenser functioning properly and ensure that the gasket provides an effective seal.

Check ranges on occasion to be sure oven vents are not blocked and to ensure that surface units are secure and level. If stove burners do not function properly, have them adjusted or replaced by a professional technician to ensure proper cooking and—in the case of gas stoves—to prevent the escape of unburned gases into the home. A well-adjusted gas flame will burn blue. A flame that's more orange than blue indicates gas that's not burning completely.

Use exhaust fans (located over stoves and ranges) when cooking to help take cooking odors, smoke, and excess moisture out of the kitchen.

Routine care of washer units includes checking the shaft seal, lubricating the pump, and tightening the belts. Such maintenance tasks often are handled as part of an annual inspection and tune-up under a service contract purchased with the appliance.

Keep dryer vents free of obstructions, including piled up snow in winter and lint build-up from the inside. Even if you clean the lint filter regularly, check the vent from time to time to be sure lint or other debris has not accumulated in the vent.

Troubleshooting

Before you call a repair service, be sure electrical appliances are plugged in and that the circuit breaker is on. If the appliance is smoking or in any way presents a danger of fire, consider the situation an emergency. *Do not throw water on an electrical fire.* If you can, throw the circuit breaker to cut power to the appliance as you exit the house (see also Fire Extinguishers).

For gas appliances with a standing pilot light, check to see if the pilot is lit; follow instructions as necessary to re-light the pilot, or—if the pilot will not remain lit—to turn off the supply of gas to the appliance. Many gas appliances now come with electric ignitions.

Attics and Attic Crawl Spaces

Attics vary greatly in size and may or may not be insulated, conditioned, or finished as part of the living area of the house. Some though not all unfinished attics and attic crawl spaces are usable for storage. If you store items in your attic keep in mind the following:

- The attic floor may not be as strong as the floors in your home's living areas.
- Heavy items may crush or compress insulation placed beneath attic flooring, reducing its effectiveness.
- Combustible or perishable items should not be stored in an attic.
- Stored items must not block necessary ventilation (for example, avoid blocking louvered openings).

Attic Ventilation

In most houses a passive ventilation system handles air exchange in the attic (Figure 7). Vents installed in the soffits draw cool air into the attic while vents near or at the ridge exhaust the warm, moist air. Soffit vents should always be unblocked; if necessary, baffles should be used to hold back any insulation that could block them.

Maintaining proper ventilation in the attic prevents warm, moist air from building up, potentially contributing to roof problems related to snow melt and ice dams (see Roofs). Even when attic space is unfinished wise homeowners check the attic once or twice a year to look for signs of water penetration and to be sure intake and exhaust vents are working properly.

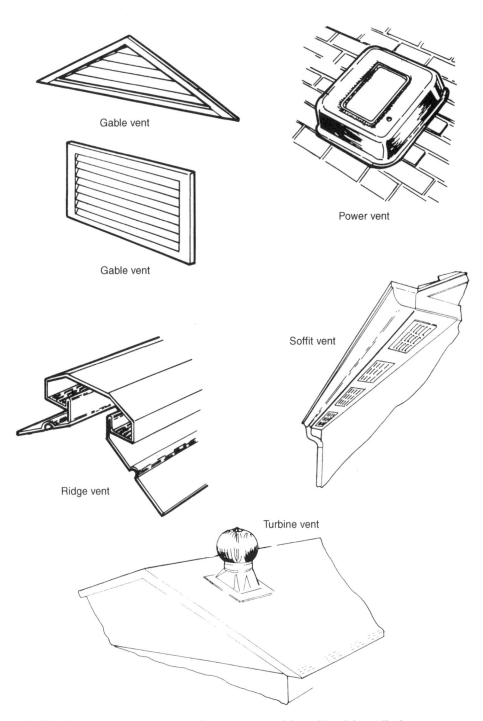

Gable vent

Gable vent

Power vent

Soffit vent

Ridge vent

Turbine vent

FIGURE 7 Various intake and exhaust vents used in residential ventilation systems.

Routine Care

Spring and autumn are logical times to schedule routine checks of the attic as the temperatures are more likely to be mild and comfortable in the unconditioned space. Make sure ventilation ports are open, airflow is unobstructed, and stored items do not block intake or exhaust vents. Check the seals where vent pipes, chimneys, attic hatches, and wiring penetrate the attic. Cracked or leaking seals allow warm, moist air to rise into the attic.

Attic Fans

Many homeowners save on air-conditioning bills (and reduce frost buildup on attic rafters and sheathing in winter) by installing a wind-activated turbine or electric attic fan. A whole-house fan quickly exhausts warm, humid, summer air (as well as irritating pollutants). Attic fans are most effective in cooling the house when the outside temperature is below 78° F.

An attic fan will operate for years with minimal maintenance. In hot weather open the windows on the lower level of the house as well as the access door to the attic. Turn on the fan (or let the wind turn the turbine) and soon you will notice a flow of air through the house. Some power fans come equipped with thermostats and humidistats.

Attic fans today are self-contained units with sealed, self-lubricating motors that require virtually no maintenance if properly installed.

Troubleshooting

Expose and seal areas where protrusions enter the wall, ceiling, or floor. For example, if a junction box for a light runs through the floor of the attic, take the faceplate off the fixture to expose the box, then apply silicone caulk or foam sealant to close any gaps.

As part of your roof maintenance routine, look around an unfinished attic for rusty nails or rust spots on insulation. These signs may indicate the presence of excess moisture in the attic. In cold weather look for frost buildup on beams, nails, and objects stored in the attic. A lingering musty smell also signals excessive moisture. Finally, if you store items in your attic, be sure they do not block the air intake or exhaust vents.

Bath and Kitchen Ventilation

Because bathrooms and kitchens are the rooms most likely to have problems with humidity and condensation, some additional points about ventilation are pertinent here. Most homeowners are naturally reluctant to bring in fresh cold air to mix with air they've already paid to heat. The best tactic then becomes reducing the humidity inside the house. Ways to reduce humidity levels in your home include:

- Check humidifier settings in winter; turn down as needed.
- Avoid hang-drying your clothing or venting clothes dryers indoors during winter. (Never vent gas dryers indoors.)
- Be sure your basement drains properly.
- Keep gutters and downspouts flowing freely.
- Maintain an appropriate slope in the ground outside basement walls.
- Cover earthen floors (such as in crawl spaces or basements) with polyethylene sheeting. Damp ground can operate like a humidifier, and crawl spaces in new homes often generate high levels of moisture.
- Use kitchen and bathroom fans to purge excess moisture while bathing and cooking.

Venting excessive moisture from bathrooms and kitchens helps reduce indoor humidity to an acceptable level. One easy solution is installing ventilation fans with humidistats that automatically run until the humidity has dropped to a preset level. Look for bathroom fans capable of 8 or more air exchanges per hour and kitchen fans capable of 15 or more air exchanges. When installing the fans, follow the manufacturer's installation instructions and use the proper size ducts to ensure the correct draw and pressure throughout the run. Minimize bends and sharp angles and secure all joints.

If you have taken all the steps listed above and still have problems with high humidity levels, check the ductwork connected to the fan(s) in the kitchen and bath. If your ductwork dead-ends in the attic, the warm, moist air it sends there will cause condensation problems when it meets with the colder air already in the attic. Rearrange the ductwork to vent through an exterior wall, a soffit, an eave, or the roof. Fittings and extensions are readily available. (See also chapter 3 for a general discussion of air circulation and ventilation; in this chapter, see Air Conditioning; also Heating Systems.)

Bathtubs, Lavatories, and Showers

Many decorative finishes in bathrooms are easily damaged by abrasive cleansers or rough scrubbing. Be sure to find out what works best on the finishes in your bathroom, read labels carefully, and test new cleaners on a small section before applying it to the entire fixture. If you received manufacturer's instructions from your builder or agent, read through them and follow the recommendations for cleaning and maintenance.

Shower and Tub Enclosures

Fiberglass, often used for tub surrounds, solves many bathroom problems. Waterproof, durable, and simple to clean, fiberglass' main drawback is a tendency to scratch when abrasive cleaners are used. Most manufacturers recommend cleaning with water and a mild dish detergent. Regular cleaning with a nonabrasive soap scum remover eliminates the need for hard scrubbing.

Cultured, synthetic, and natural marble sheeting is easy to clean. Cultured marble requires diligent care because it cannot be resurfaced. Acrylic finishes make cultured marble sturdier and longer lasting. Synthetic marble is a tough material; scratches, abrasions, and even burns often can be repaired with fine-grade sandpaper.

Plastic Laminates come in many colors, patterns, and textures, including wood and marble look-alikes. Laminates resist water and stains and clean easily with soap and water or nonabrasive cleaners. Nonabrasive cleaners keep the laminate from dulling and wearing thin. Laminates can chip or dent if hit hard enough.

Bathtubs

Fiberglass-reinforced plastic feels warmer to the touch than many other materials. Most tubs made from this material weigh between 60 and 70 pounds and are sturdily reinforced. Although this material doesn't chip easily, abrasive cleaners will mar the surface.

Molded cast iron with a porcelain enamel finish makes an extraordinarily durable tub weighing from 350 to 500 pounds. Cast iron keeps water warm for a long time. Although porcelain enamel stands up to scrubbing better than fiberglass, it eventually wears thin. Always use a nonabrasive cleanser.

Formed steel tubs, also with a porcelain enamel finish, offer a less expensive alternative to cast iron and are not nearly so heavy, weighing usually between 120 and 125 pounds. Formed steel tubs do not retain heat as long as fiberglass or cast iron tubs and are prone to chipping and denting. Use a nonabrasive cleanser.

Lavatories

Porcelainized cast iron lavatories are extraordinarily durable but very heavy, requiring a sturdy support system. Enameled steel doesn't wear as well but is considerably lighter than cast iron. Stainless steel is light, durable, and unaffected by most commercial household chemicals. The steel tends to collect spots from hard water and soap residue, however, requiring more frequent cleaning with a soap scum or lime scale remover.

Vitreous china is easy to clean and has a lustrous surface but can crack or chip if hit with a heavy object. Fiberglass-reinforced plastic can be molded into novel shapes, but it won't hold a shine as well as other surfaces and requires frequent cleaning. Marbleized china has all the sterling qualities of the best natural china, but also chips and breaks easily like natural china. Simulated or cultured marble is handsome, but abrasive cleaners may spoil the finish.

Self-rimming (or surface-mounted) lavatories feature a ridge around the bowl that fits over the countertop to form a tight seal. The ridge prevents water from splashing onto the counter. Flush-mounted lavatories recess into the countertop with a tight-fitting metal rim around the bowl. The rim comes in different finishes to match the faucet. Flush-mounted lavatories may allow water to escape onto the counter, making the rim joint hard to clean. Recessed lavatories fit into a cutout on the countertop. These lavatories also can be difficult to clean around the edge. One-piece integral lavatories are molded with no joint or separation between the bowl and countertop, eliminating the possibility of leakage.

Routine Care

Cleaning and prevention of stains in bathtubs, showers, and lavatories will be much easier if you avoid high-risk habits. Avoid the following:

- letting food wastes stand in a bathroom or kitchen sink
- using sinks or tubs to hold paint cans, trash, or tools when you are redecorating
- wearing shoes in a bathtub when cleaning or redecorating—the grit on the soles of the shoes will scratch the surface
- using photographic or developing solutions in bathtubs or bathroom sinks (The stains from such chemicals are very difficult to remove.)
- leaving metal utensils (including scouring pads) in the sink

Protect surfaces that are easily dented or chipped by placing furniture or decorative elements away from the sink or tub (to prevent bumping) and by placing hammers or other tools on the floor when redecorating. When painting or redecorating in a bathroom, cover sinks, tubs, and fixtures to protect them against paint drips. If you must remove dried paint using a razor blade, always angle the blade so that it skims across and does not dig into the surface.

Observe the caulking around the rims of tubs and lavatories from time to time. Remove dried caulk and replace it by running a thin bead of caulk all around and pressing it into the cavity between the sink or tub and the wall using your finger, a pencil, or another thin object. Fill the bathtub with water before applying the new caulk. The weight of the water positions the tub so the gap is at its maximum and—once caulked—the seal is more complete.

Troubleshooting

To eliminate mildew, keep moisture levels down in the bathroom by using the exhaust fan during baths and showers and by wiping down tiles, tubs, and shower enclosures after bathing or showering. Spread out damp towels and washcloths to allow moisture to evaporate faster. Clean mildewed areas with a nonaerosol spray mildew remover, rinse and dry, then use a disinfectant to retard regrowth and eliminate odors.

Special cleaners are available to remove stains that metals and hard water (mineral) deposits can leave in sinks and tubs. But such cleaners can be harsh and dull surfaces—check compatibility before using such cleaners on your sink or tub.

▷ **Brick—See Masonry**

Carbon Monoxide Detectors

Carbon monoxide is a colorless, odorless, tasteless, and deadly gas produced when fossil fuels are not burned completely. Properly installed and maintained appliances burn fossil fuels cleanly, producing only trace amounts of carbon monoxide. The risk of carbon monoxide poisoning increases dramatically when homeowners use kerosene, oil, or liquid propane space heaters without taking steps to provide adequate ventilation.

Types of Detectors

Carbon monoxide detectors can be battery operated, hard-wired, or require no external power source at all. Small, inexpensive detection cards imprinted with a chemical can be placed around the house. The chemical dot changes color when carbon monoxide is present, but the homeowner must notice the color change. Remember to replace detection cards with new cards as instructed on the packaging. Hard-wired and plug-in detectors last longer and require little attention after installation, but do not operate during power outages. Battery-operated detectors are attractive because they are easy to install and will operate during power outages.

Place carbon monoxide detectors in the major living spaces of the house, especially bedrooms, and near fossil fuel-burning appliances. If possible, locate detectors at least 15 feet from the furnace, hot water heater, or cooking appliances to guard against false alarms. Always read and follow the installation instructions furnished with the detector.

Routine Care

Carbon monoxide detectors need regular cleaning to keep them free of accumulated dust, dirt, and insect buildup. Battery-operated units and hard-wired units with battery backup require new batteries twice a year. Battery-operated units may also need a new sensor annually. Read the manufacturer's manual to ensure proper maintenance and performance.

Responding to an Alarm

Symptoms of carbon monoxide poisoning include confusion, irrational thinking, memory loss, and fatigue. If your carbon monoxide detector sounds the alarm and you are experiencing these symptoms, immediately evacuate the residence, then call 911. If you are not experiencing poisoning symptoms, open windows and doors to ventilate the house. Turn off potential sources of the leak and press the reset button (if your detector has one). If the alarm sounds again contact a professional for an immediate home inspection to track down the source. Do not ignore the alarm. These detectors experience few, if any, false alarms.

Carpeting

Carpeting, a preferred floor covering for decades, remains a mainstay in most homes in the United States. Carpeting is warm and comfortable to walk on, but tends to retain moisture and dirt within its fibers.

Special grades of carpeting are available for use in high-moisture areas such as kitchens and bathrooms. This carpet is mildew resistant, less susceptible to water soaking and staining, and does not retain odors. Indoor-outdoor carpet can be quite rugged, and styles today are more varied than ever before.

Carpeting comes in a wide range of styles and materials, each with its own strengths and drawbacks. Generally carpeting will either come with an attached backing material or be installed over a separate backing layer. This layer adds to the cushioning effect and helps protect the fibers from being crushed. If you are planning to repair or replace a section of carpet, be sure to consider the underlayers when making your measurements and pricing your purchase.

Routine Care

Most carpeting requires little routine care other than regular (weekly) vacuuming, prompt cleanup of spills, and occasional spot treatment. Depending on the color and the material, some carpeting may fade over time if exposed to direct sunlight. Choosing colors and materials carefully to suit each room and (when appropriate) shielding carpeting and upholstery fabrics by keeping blinds or curtains drawn helps reduce the likelihood of fading. Homeowners can further protect carpeting and prolong its life by:

- using furniture rests under legs of chairs, couches, and other heavy objects that rest on the carpet
- periodically rearranging furniture, which modifies the traffic patterns in a room
- placing area rugs over the carpeting in high-traffic areas, such as entryways
- using cleaners and stain removers that are compatible with the carpet fabric, and testing new cleaners in an out-of-the-way spot before applying them to the entire carpet

Candle wax drippings can be difficult to remove from carpeting, but good results can be obtained by placing a plan (unwaxed) paper bag over the area and holding a warm iron against the paper. The iron should be warm but not too hot; as the heat melts the wax, it will seep into the paper. Repeat using different parts of the bag or additional bags, blotting up as much was as possible. Scrape remaining wax residue from carpet fibers using a dull knife. When blotting and scraping wax, try to avoid driving the wax farther into the pile.

For cleaning purposes, it's not advisable to permanently install carpeting around bathroom fixtures. Simply fit the carpeting around the fixtures, allowing it to lay loose. Lift the carpeting when necessary to clean areas around the fixtures and replace it after the floor and fixtures are dry.

▶ **Ceilings—See Walls**

Ceiling Fans

Ceiling fans make use of warm air's tendency to rise and cold air's tendency to fall. Depending on the direction in which the fan turns, the paddles either pull heavier, cold air up from the floor into the living space during summer months or push lighter, warm air from the ceiling back down into the living space during winter months. A small switch, usually located on the paddle hub, will change the paddle direction.

Using paddle fans can greatly improve your comfort, reduce utility bills, and increase the efficiency of your heating and air-conditioning system. Properly installed, ceiling fans require minimal care (occasional dusting, replacement of bulbs in units with lamps).

Chimneys, Fireplaces, and Wood-Burning Appliances

Manufacturers continue to make advances in home heating with appliances that burn wood and wood byproducts. With specially designed firebrick, fireboxes, air intakes, and blower systems, newer appliances generate from 38,000 Btu to 55,000 Btu of heat depending on the model.

Newer generations of fireplaces, woodstoves, and other wood-burning appliances also can be installed in a wider variety of locations. Some appliances use specially engineered vent ducts and no longer require a conventional chimney.

Chimneys and Conventional Fireplaces

Believe it or not, your chimney contributes to your home's air exchange system simply because it provides a conduit for hotter air to rise and cooler air to fall. During warm weather, heavy, humid air can actually flow down the chimney into your home. You can adjust the damper to control how much air flows in and out of the house.

When operating the fireplace, always make sure that the damper is open, allowing smoke to freely flow up the chimney. Otherwise, keep the damper closed and the warm indoor air inside. Don't forget the chimney when a storm approaches. Depending on the anticipated changes in air pressure, you may want to close the flue to prevent wind gusts from blowing soot into your house or open it to help the indoor air pressure equalize with the changes outside, thus preventing potential damage to windows.

If you have a gas fireplace, less routine care is generally required. Follow the manufacturer's instructions. If the fireplace design includes a direct vent to the outside rather than a chimney, keep the flue or vent open at all times—

even when the fireplace is not being used. Do not smoke cigarettes or cigars while cleaning or lighting the fireplace. If you smell leaking gas leave immediately and call your gas company from somewhere outside the house.

Wood-Burning Stoves and Pellet-Burning Appliances

Wood-burning stoves are typically made of metal, usually cast iron, although ceramic stoves with polymer coatings are now available.

Generally, the larger and heavier the stove, the more heat it will hold, allowing it to radiate warmth long after the fire has died out. Vents in the stove control how much draft enters the combustion chamber. By properly controlling the draft, you can maintain a fire for many hours on a single load of wood.

Wood-burning stoves come in several varieties. Free-standing stoves can be placed anywhere with access to an outside wall for the chimney (see Figure 8). Free-standing stoves need to rest on an appropriate pad or apron.

Fireplace inserts are another option. This form of wood stove mounts inside a conventional fireplace and uses the chimney as access for its own chimney. Part of the stove extends into the room. Most fireboxes have a small metal plate that opens onto a chute, allowing you to dispose of ashes. (Spread the ashes around your flowerbeds; they add natural nutrients to the soil.)

Glass doors often are used with both conventional fireplaces and fireplace inserts. Glass doors and the air vents above and below them control the airflow into and out of the firebox. Once the fire is completely extinguished, close off these air vents to prevent the flow of warm air up the chimney.

FIGURE 8 Example of a free-standing wood-burning stove.

Pellet stoves, known more commonly as pellet-fired appliances, or PFAs, produce an abundance of heat with a minimum of ash and virtually no sulfur or creosote emissions to foul the air. In fact, some states' environmental restrictions prohibit the use of wood stoves or fireplaces on days when air quality is poor. Clean-burning PFAs are exempt from all such EPA regulations. And a typical PFA produces up to 50,000 Btu of heat, enough to warm a 2,400 square-foot home.

Pellet-fired appliances resemble wood stoves with some notable exceptions. The pellets (made from ground and compressed sawdust, scrap wood, or even nutshells) are poured from 40-pound bags. Usually one filling per day will suffice, depending on the desired temperature. An internal auger automatically feeds the correct amount of pellets into the burning chamber throughout the day (see Figure 9). The pellets are sold by the ton, and a typical home uses one to three tons of pellets per year.

Routine Care

Each fall, inspect the condition of fireplaces, chimneys, and wood-burning appliances before using them for the first time. Open and close dampers to make sure they operate smoothly and without obstruction. Use a mirror and flashlight to examine the condition of the fireplace masonry and to look up the chimney past the flue. The mirror will make it possible to see all surfaces of the chimney.

Check the chimney for birds' nests or other obstructions that could ignite or block the escape of smoke. Check for glassy-looking creosote (soot) deposits. Every year creosote deposits ignite and cause many house fires.

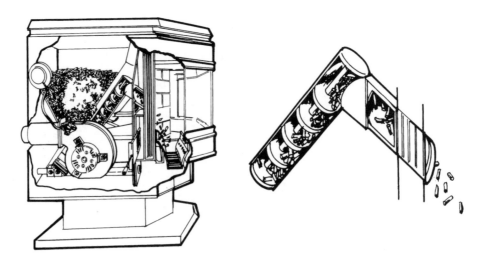

FIGURE 9 Left: An example of a pellet-fired appliance and its components. Right: An auger inside a pellet-fired appliance automatically stokes the fire.

Look for cracks in the bricks, which can allow moisture to penetrate walls from the chimney shaft and also cause drafts. Drafts can suck flames and smoke back into the cracks, potentially igniting combustible construction materials behind the brick.

In spring prepare for the air-conditioning season by cleaning the fireplace area and closing off the flue.

The type and condition of wood burned in the fireplace directly affects the amount of residue left inside of the chimney. Hardwoods, such as maple or cherry, burn cleaner than softwoods. Softwoods like pine will burn quickly and contain a lot of tar and resin that do not burn off before smoke and flames carry them up the chimney. The tar and resin then attach to the cooler brick as they travel up the chimney.

Wood that is improperly seasoned (dried out) produces an abundance of smoke; and the more smoke, the more residue. Use only well-seasoned wood. Manmade logs and gas fireplaces with artificial logs actually emit less contaminant particulate matter than natural wood logs. Electing to have a gas fireplace or to burn manmade logs reduces soot production and helps you maintain better indoor air quality. Be sure to use the andirons or grate; do not build fires directly on the fireplace floor.

Have the fireplace professionally cleaned by a chimney sweep after every two cords of wood burned. The chimney sweep will also inspect the condition of the chimney cap and the flashing around the chimney where it penetrates the roof. The inspection should also include checking the firebox and making sure the damper is properly operating.

Wood-burning stoves and pellet-fired appliances usually need a yearly professional cleaning by a chimney sweep. Visually inspect and regularly clean your wood-burning stove, fireplace, or pellet stove.

Circuit Breakers and Your Home's Electrical System

Think of a circuit breaker as a heat-sensing, spring-loaded switch with three states—*on, off,* and *tripped* (see Figure 10). The tripped position is not the same as the off position: you will find the toggle switch on the circuit breaker in the tripped position only if the circuit has overloaded or experienced a short.

When the circuit switch is on, current flows through a set of contacts held together by a spring and lever. These are kept in tension by a bimetal strip that also carries current as part of the circuit. If the circuit develops a short or an overload, the bimetal strip heats up and bends, causing the spring to separate the contacts and interrupt the flow of current. When the current stops, the bimetal cools and tries to straighten again. The strip is not strong enough to stretch the spring, however, so the contacts remain open until you reset the toggle switch.

Before working on a circuit (installing a new outlet, for instance) you must locate the correct circuit breaker for that outlet and flip the toggle switch to the off position.

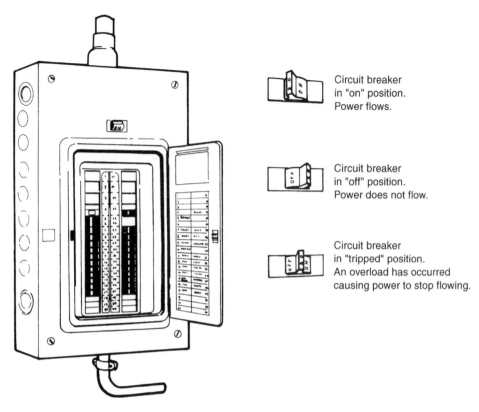

Circuit breaker in "on" position. Power flows.

Circuit breaker in "off" position. Power does not flow.

Circuit breaker in "tripped" position. An overload has occurred causing power to stop flowing.

FIGURE 10 A typical breaker box has individual switches controlling each circuit. Each switch has three distinct settings.

Outlets and Switches

When current flows to a wall outlet or switch, the electrons travel inside a hot wire. After current has flowed through a device (such as a lamp, stereo, or other appliance) the electrons seek a direct route to the ground, traveling inside neutral wires to get there. Neutral wires, also known as *system grounds,* complete every circuit in the system by returning current to the ground. By convention hot wires are generally black; neutral wires, white.

Circuits now usually include a third bare or green wire that serves as an *equipment ground* that protects against the danger of short circuits. The third prong on the three-pronged plugs used for major appliances connects to the equipment ground.

Routine Care

Circuit breakers need little routine care. In fact, most homeowners only attend to their home's circuit breakers in response to a problem such as a tripped circuit. It makes sense, however, to take some simple precautionary steps to ensure safe and proper operation of circuit breakers:

- Keep the area in front of the breaker box free of obstructions such as storage boxes, tools, and so forth.
- Make sure the circuits in the box are clearly labeled.
- Have your builder or electrician explain how the system is grounded. The ground may run into the earth outside your house; if so, know the location of the ground so you do not disturb it.

Troubleshooting

If the same circuit breaker trips over and over again, chances are you have overloaded the circuit. One way to prevent overloaded circuits is to calculate an amp rating for each electrical device in your house. First, list the amperage requirements of every electrical appliance and device served by each outlet or switch in your home. (Amperage requirements often are noted on a permanent label or printed directly on the electrical wire close to the plug. If the figure is given in watts, just divide it by 120 to determine the amperage.) Second, note which circuit serves each outlet and switch. Third, add up all the amperage figures for each circuit. Finally, compare that total against the amperage capacity listed on the appropriate breaker.

Most circuits are 120 volts and general-purpose circuits usually require 15-amp breakers. At least two 20-amp small appliance circuits should be available for the kitchen. Heavy appliances such as washing machines and clothes dryers normally have their own heavy-duty circuit with a larger capacity circuit breaker.

When you have completed your evaluation, you'll know for sure whether any particular circuit would face an overload if every device tied into it were to call for current at the same time.

Ground Fault Circuit Interrupters (GFCIs): Misinformation and misunderstandings surrounding GFCIs still seem to confuse some homeowners. A ground fault circuit interrupter (GFCI) is designed to prevent electrical shocks to people. It is not designed to protect a circuit from overload (as fuses and circuit breakers do). GFCIs also do not protect circuits and appliances from electrical surges (as surge suppressors do).

A GFCI works by monitoring the current in both the hot and neutral lines connected to it. The level should always be equal. A drop in current in the neutral line means that some of the current is being siphoned off, or grounded. A GFCI reacts instantly to changes in current as little as 1/200th of an ampere. This means that, should a person inadvertently become the ground for a circuit the GFCI will cut, or "interrupt" the circuit before the person even feels a shock. GFCIs add a measure of safety in locations such as kitchens, bathrooms, or utility rooms where people both use water and handle multiple appliances.

GFCIs are now considered acceptable substitutes for two-pronged outlets where no ground is available, a common situation in many older homes. Installing GFCIs can be a less-expensive alternative to installing grounds for each of the home's outlets.

Should your survey reveal some overloaded circuits several remedies are available. You may be able to add circuits, shuffle outlets from one circuit to another, or do a little of both.

When you're through listing the circuits and appliances in your house, post a copy of the list next to or inside the door of your service panel. At a glance you'll be able to see which breaker to flip when you need to work on an outlet or switch.

Cleaning Exterior and Interior Surfaces

Aside from keeping up appearances, regularly cleaning your home's exterior and interior surfaces encourages a thorough inspection of exterior finishes, slows deterioration caused by accumulated grime and debris, helps protect the structural integrity of the house, and supports the resale value of your investment.

The exteriors of many new homes now incorporate aluminum or vinyl products together with brick, stone, or stucco. Such materials often require little or no painting; however, all home exteriors benefit from periodic cleaning. And with traditional wood siding routine maintenance, cleaning, and touch-up painting can help extend the life of a paint job (see Painting).

General Cleaning of Exterior Surfaces

Many specialty products are available to clean and remove stains from wood, masonry, cement, and glass. A detailed review of these products is beyond the scope of this book. However, by reading product labels carefully, selecting appropriate products, and following product manufacturers' instructions for their use and disposal you will help protect the finishes on the exterior of your home and also protect your soil and landscaping.

Many homeowners use power washers, which enable them to work from the ground and cover large areas of the house relatively quickly. Home power washing units are available that connect to the garden hose. More powerful units are available at equipment rental centers.

Before power washing, especially with more powerful units, check to be sure elements of the siding, shutters, and trim have not worked loose, and to be sure windows are closed. (If exterior paint has begun to peel, the force of the water may strip away paint along with surface dirt and grime.) It's a good idea to walk around the house for an all-over check before beginning, and to double-check each surface section as you prepare to wash it. Use a horizontal motion when directing the spray in order to avoid knocking loose the locking mechanism that holds siding courses together. Avoid spraying gutters and downspouts with a high-pressure stream; it is too easy to knock them loose and cause damage. For similar reasons, avoid accidentally directing the spray full force against window glass. Finally, be sure to flood the cleaned area with clean water after washing.

General Cleaning of Interior Surfaces

Periodic deep cleaning of interior surfaces will help keep your home in tip-top shape. It also can keep you healthier by reducing the levels of indoor pollutants that may aggravate illnesses or allergies. Many people schedule a heavy-duty spring cleaning once or twice a year, usually in the spring or autumn, sometimes both.

Areas that collect dust or that are warm and moist are breeding grounds for biological pollutants such as pollens, viruses, bacteria, and pet dander. Regularly clean areas such as:

- behind and under large appliances (remove the grille on the front and vacuum)
- bathrooms, particularly behind toilets and under sinks
- kitchen floors, walls, and ceilings
- humidifiers, particularly portable units
- major appliances such as furnaces, heat pumps, and central air conditioners

Change air filters for heating and cooling systems frequently according to the manufacturer's directions (see also Air-Conditioning Systems; Filters; and Heating Systems).

Household Chemicals and Alternative Products

We live in an age of chemicals, which sometimes leads us to take for granted that the products we buy to control pests or to clean, polish, or preserve the various materials and products in our home are safe and easy to use. However, responsible use, storage, and disposal of household chemicals can take some thought. Most chemical products are safe if handled properly; but many homeowners fail to read the instructions and observe the warnings printed on the labels of common household products. Mishandling of household chemicals can cause unnecessary property damage and it also can be dangerous to your health.

Always use household chemicals according to the manufacturer's instructions and under well-ventilated conditions. If you must, open a window in winter. If recommended for the product, use gloves and wear eye protection.

Avoid mixing different products—including different brands of the same product. Depending on the products, doing so could cause an explosive chemical reaction or create toxic gases. If you spill a hazardous chemical, sprinkle it with sawdust, vermiculite, or cat box litter, then sweep it into a plastic garbage bag. Dispose of it as hazardous waste, making sure the material does not come into contact with your skin or eyes.

Many yard- and home-care products including fertilizers, insecticides, herbicides, paints, stains, sealers, and cleaning solutions contain chemicals that are poisonous to humans and pets. Dry chemicals may lose their effectiveness if they absorb too much moisture. Liquids will evaporate if kept in open containers. Store all chemical products in the original packaging. If the packaging is damaged, place it in a sealable plastic container. Store petroleum products, paint, or cleaning products in a cool, dry location locked away from children and pets, and keep the following pointers in mind:

- Buy household chemicals in quantities sufficient to meet your immediate needs without requiring long-term storage.
- The original labels provide directions for proper use, disposal suggestions, and warnings. Keep them intact.
- Keep unused products in their original containers. Never store chemicals in food or beverage containers.
- Store flammable products away from living quarters. Keep flammable substances in a separate storage facility away from the living space and away from ignition sources such as appliances with pilot lights. Once opened, containers may emit vapors that pose a hazard even if the chemical itself does not come in contact with a flame. Also, some aerosol products may pose a risk of explosion should a fire occur.

Follow the directions on the label when disposing of chemical products or their containers. Don't simply put them in the trash or dump them where they can contaminate food or water resources. Household trash is often placed in landfills where chemicals or fertilizers can leak into the ground, potentially contaminating groundwater. Contact your local municipality; many local governments schedule special collection days to dispose of chemicals or other potentially hazardous items. Other localities designate special drop-off locations for hazardous materials. If no program exists in your area, contact local refuse companies for information on how to safely dispose of these items.

If you are sensitive to chemicals or simply prefer to minimize your use of commercial chemicals, alternative cleaning and pest-control products and techniques may appeal to you. Try these common recipes to combat the following problems:

- Ants: Pour a line of cream of tartar or chili powder where ants enter the house. They won't cross the line. Outside, pour boiling water over ant nests.
- Cockroaches: Store food in airtight containers. Caulk all cracks in walls and spaces between baseboards and walls and place bay leaves nearby. Combine boric acid powder with a small amount of water to make a sticky substance you can use as a trap. Set out a dish containing equal parts of oatmeal and plaster of Paris.
- Fleas and ticks: Feed your pets brewer's yeast and garlic. Vacuum pet bedding regularly. Place eucalyptus seeds, leaves, and cedar chips near pet bedding.

- Moths: Set cedar chips, cedar blocks, or lavender flowers around closets. Wrap wool clothing in plastic bags during warm weather. A cedar closet is ideal for storing wool.
- Stains on fabric: Dab old, set stains with white vinegar. Sponge up brand-new stains or scrape off the offending material as much as possible. Using a clean (preferably white) cloth, dab the area with club soda followed by cold water.
- Butter, gravy, chocolate, or urine stains: Dab with a solution of 1 teaspoon white vinegar and 1 quart cold water.
- Fresh grease stains: Dab with a damp cloth dipped in Borax. Or apply a paste of cornstarch and water; let it dry and brush the mixture off.
- Ink stains: Apply a cream of tartar and lemon juice mixture using a wet cloth. Let the mixture sit for one hour, then wash in the usual manner.
- Red wine spills: Clean immediately with club soda, or dab out excess moisture with an absorbent cloth and sprinkle salt on the stain. Let the salt stand several hours, then brush or vacuum.

When treating all types of stains, use a dabbing motion, not vigorous rubbing, lest you work the stain further into the fabric or damage the weave. The following additional alternative cleaning mixtures are recommended by the Center for Hazardous Materials Research (CHMR):

- Scouring powder: Apply a solution of vinegar, salt, and water or baking soda and water, then sponge and rinse clean.
- Toilet bowl cleaner: Pour 1/2 cup white vinegar and 3 tablespoons baking soda into the toilet bowl, let stand for 30 minutes, then scrub with a long-handled brush and flush.
- Ceramic tile cleaner: Mix 1/4 cup of white vinegar into a gallon of warm water. Apply with a sponge.
- Disinfectants: Use 1/2 cup Borax dissolved in hot water. Apply with a sponge. Use sodium carbonate in the clothes washer.
- Air fresheners or deodorizers: Sprinkle baking soda in odor-producing areas. Set vinegar out in an open dish. Sprinkle Borax in corners. Sprinkle baking soda over carpeting and vacuum after 30 minutes.
- Oven cleaner: Scrub with a paste of baking soda, salt, and water. Then leave 1/4 cup lemon juice in the oven overnight and wipe away any remaining grease the next morning. (Ventilate the kitchen and avoid breathing fumes.)
- Oven-spill remover: Sprinkle salt on the spill immediately. Let the oven cool a few minutes, then scrape the spill away and wash the area clean.
- Window and glass cleaner: Measure 3 tablespoons lime juice, 1 tablespoon white vinegar, and 3/4 cup water into a clean spray bottle. Spray on window, wipe clean, and dry with newspaper.

Computerized Systems—See Home Automation

Condensation—See Foundations; also Windows

Decks and Platforms

Wooden decks and platforms can offer a casual extension of living and entertaining space for many years.

Many different finishes are available for wooden decks and platforms. The finish you choose will depend on the decking material and your personal preference. Some people enjoy the natural weathered look of cedar and redwood, but if left unfinished these woods can weather unevenly and suffer from mildew and other problems. Over time, however, moisture from rain or melting snow can penetrate the wood on a deck or platform, especially at board ends and joints, causing rot.

Bleaching stains give cedar and redwood a more evenly weathered appearance and contain protective additives. Penetrating stains offer a natural appearance and protection from moisture. The stains penetrate the wood, eliminate the peeling or blistering commonly seen on painted exteriors. Stains perform well on areas exposed to severe weather and on knotty or textured woods. Most stains contain water repellents and some also contain rot and mildew inhibitors.

Penetrating stains come in three types: transparent, semitransparent and opaque. Transparent stains contain no pigments but have water-repellent features that protect the wood without hiding the natural coloration and slow the natural process of color change. Semi-transparent stains contain some pigment and may slightly modify or obscure wood's characteristic grain and knots. Semi-transparent stains tend to be much more durable than transparent stains. Opaque stains are high in pigment content, thoroughly hide the grain and color of the wood, and perform much like paint. If you prefer a painted look, use an opaque stain or choose an exterior latex or alkyd-based paint.

Deck stains or coatings penetrate best when the wood has dried to a moisture content below 20 percent and the air temperature during application is between 50° F and 80° F. Newly installed decks may need to dry for several months before they are ready to accept a stain. If the surface you plan to stain will soak up a few drops of water, the wood is dry enough to apply stain or deck preservatives.

Natural bristle brushes are the best tools for applying stain, paint, or water repellents to decking. Maintain a wet edge between brush strokes to prevent lap marks. Start at a finished area and brush toward the wet edge. Sealant also can be applied with spraying equipment. Check the directions on the stain or water repellent for specific application details.

Routine Care

Regular maintenance to preserve your deck or platform involves the following steps:

- Regularly sweep the deck or platform clear of dirt and leaves.
- Once or twice each season, scrub away any collected dirt.

- Scrape and sand areas of peeling paint.
- Recoat the deck with a sealer, preservative, stain, or paint as desired when the finish begins to show signs of wear.
- Check the deck at least once a year for popped nails, loose screws or bolts.
- As necessary, replace weak, spongy decking or supporting members with strong new wood of the same size and type.
- Check structural members for signs of moisture damage and decay. Posts, beams, and joists are particularly prone to rot, particularly areas that are hidden by the decking.

Troubleshooting

If mildew appears, scrub stained areas with a mixture of water and household bleach, or use a specialized product to remove green or black mildew stains and prohibit future growth.

Remove food stains such as barbecue sauce and grease with an automotive degreaser. Use this kind of degreaser only when the area to be cleaned is shaded.

Treat oily leaf stains with household bleach diluted one-to-one with water. For extreme cases, full-strength bleach may be necessary.

Control green moss or algae stains by scrubbing hard with a full-strength bleach solution. These stains can be difficult to remove and almost always reappear because the plants form a root structure in the wood.

Remove sap stains using turpentine and a stiff brush. Remove brown or black rust spots from nails, furniture, or toys by applying a 5 percent solution of oxalic acid mixed in water. One application should remove about 90 percent of the stain; a second application should raise that to 99 percent of the stain. Oxalic acid is a kind of wood bleach available in most hardware stores.

Whenever you apply a bleach or other stain-removing solution to wooden decking or platform elements, be sure to rinse the area well and allow the wood time to dry before applying restorer or wood sealer. Following use of a bleach solution, use a deck restorer to bring back the natural color of the wood.

Doors

Exterior doors, interior doors, garage doors, storm doors—doors vary in design, function, and complexity. All provide points of transition from one space to another in the home. Some emphasize security, others privacy, and still others emphasize access and light.

Storm doors, like storm windows, provide considerable protection from outside temperatures. Most people think of storm windows and doors as a way of keeping out cold winter temperatures; but in warmer climates and during summer months storm doors and windows also help keep colder, air-conditioned air inside the house. Storm doors also can reduce the amount of dust that enters the house, particularly from street-facing windows and doors, and reduce overall wear on materials that would otherwise be exposed directly to the elements.

The life expectancies and maintenance needs of doors vary with the materials, placement, and functions of the door. Most can be expected to last for several decades, and if protected from weathering, some doors may last for the lifetime of the house.

Routine Care

Each spring and autumn, examine and operate each door to be sure the door swings freely on its hinges and that all hardware, particularly latches and locks, are functioning properly (see also Home Security). Check the following:

- weepholes in storm doors to be sure they are not blocked
- screens and screen panels, making repairs during the off season
- wooden doors, for signs of warping caused by moisture and changing temperatures
- thresholds and metal tracks, for signs of weather damage
- metal or plastic weatherstripping, regluing or renailing when you observe signs of wear (see Weatherstripping)
- painted surfaces, including doorframes
- all surfaces, removing accumulated dirt and grime

If the door or doorframe contains glass panels, use caution when applying glass cleaners—the ammonia in many glass cleaning products will remove the shine from gloss paints. If you use an ammonia-based cleaner spray the cleaner onto a cloth or paper towel and then wipe the glass. Clean painted, stained, or varnished wood surfaces using a solution of mild soap and water followed by a thorough rinsing with clean water. Sweep sills and thresholds using a stiff broom to remove excess water that remains after cleaning. (If left to air-dry the water may leave small amounts of soap residue that attract dirt.)

Repaint wooden doors when the house or trim is painted, approximately every four to six years. Oil the moving parts of garage doors every three months and check and tighten screws that fasten door hinges and hardware once a year.

Troubleshooting

Sticking is a frequent problem with doors. When you have a door that sticks, try to diagnose the underlying problem: Has a hinge worked loose? Has the door swelled because of damp weather? If necessary, fold sandpaper around a wooden block and sand the edge of the door where it sticks. (If sanding is insufficient, you may use a plane to further shave back the edge—but go cautiously and don't overdo it.) Repaint or varnish sanded or planed areas promptly to prevent further moisture penetration.

If a wooden door has become warped, try removing it from the frame and thoroughly drying it in the sun. If necessary, apply weights to the bulged side, leaving the weights in place for two or three days. (Watch the weather forecast for a suitable block of sunny days with no threat of rain.)

▶ **Driveways, Walks, and Steps—See Paved Surfaces**

▶ **Electrical Outlets and Switches—See Circuit Breakers**

▶ **Faucets and Drains—See Plumbing**

Filters

The two types of filters likely to be present in your home are air-cleaning filters and water filters. By capturing dirt or impurities filters help protect equipment such as furnaces or water heaters. Filters also contribute to a more pleasant and healthy indoor environment.

Furnace and Air-Cleaning Filters

Most disposable or washable furnace filters are made of paper, cloth, wire mesh, or a combination of those materials. Such filters keep large particles, including bugs, hair, and lint balls, out of the home heating, ventilation, and air-conditioning (HVAC) system. They are generally rated between 3 and 8 percent efficient at catching small particles 5 microns in size.

Most furnace manufacturers recommend changing disposable filters monthly and cleaning washable filters almost as frequently to prevent dirt buildup and straining of the system. One easy way to flush dirt from washable filters is using the pressure nozzle on the end of a garden hose. It is important to get into the habit of changing or cleaning furnace filters regularly, especially when making the transition between heating and cooling seasons.

Higher density air filters can reduce surface grime. Filtering the air makes it easier to keep walls, floors, and other surfaces clean. Some filters are designed to control odors and capture plant pollens, spores, and dusts responsible for common allergies. The more efficient filters can even reduce the particulate allergens present in tobacco smoke. These filters are rated 30 to 45 percent efficient at trapping particles as small as 1/2 micron. They also are available in both disposable and cleanable varieties.

Air-cleaning and filtration systems can be purchased as standalone units or built in as part of a home's HVAC system. The most common air cleaners are:

- filter systems that use a medium (fabric) similar to a typical furnace filter
- electronic air cleaners, also called electrostatic precipitators, that trap electrically charged particles using an opposing electrical field
- a variety of hybrid devices blending filter media and electronic technology

For people with allergies or sensitivity to chemicals and for rooms with a particularly high level of airborne pollutants—craft or hobby rooms, for example—standalone units can help supplement a central air-cleaning system.

The most effective air filters are electronic air cleaners, also known as electrostatic air cleaners. These are 75 to 95 percent effective at reducing airborne particles as small as 1/1000 of a micron.

Plan to clean an electrostatic filter at least four times a year. The filter usually rests in the air-handling unit with a pre-filter on either side (Figure 11). You can remove the pre-filters by pulling them straight toward you. The main component, consisting of two electronic cells, is held in place with top and bottom plates with handles on them. Pull the main filter unit straight out toward you.

Use a hose and high-pressure nozzle to thoroughly wash the main filter on both sides. Allow it to drain, then stand the filter up on the opposite end to check for trapped water. The filter should completely dry in 30 to 45 minutes. Don't forget to wash the pre-filters as well.

Water Filters

If your well water or local water supplies are high in dissolved mineral salts, sediment, or contaminants, the water may smell or taste of sulfur or be gray-colored. Incoming water may be gritty, cause an orange-colored residue, or even turn fixtures black. Deposits in the water can also create *scale,* which shortens the life of your water heater and pipes.

Most of the water problems described above can be resolved or improved by using filters, softeners, or distillers. Water filtration or treatment systems are more often used with rural well water.

A variety of affordable filtration systems use replaceable cores to treat a multitude of problems. Some filters trap sediment while others screen out specific

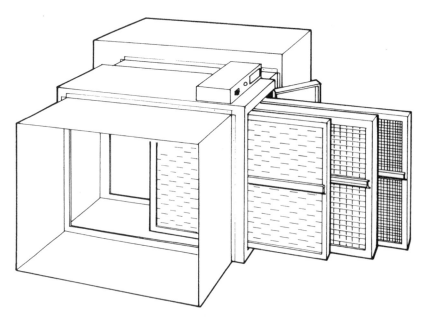

FIGURE 11 A typical electrostatic filter arrangement and placement.

minerals such as iron or manganese. Granular carbon filters effectively remove many organic and inorganic contaminants. If traces of soluble iron threaten your pipes and fixtures, a phosphate crystal filter will correct much of the piping problem while sweetening your tap water. If you live near a mountain stream containing *Giardia* (a microorganism that causes severe flu-like symptoms), there is even a filter to keep Giardia cysts out of your water system.

If you discover that your water contains any biological or chemical contaminants, check with local health officials about recommended solutions. Simple and affordable water testing kits are available in many hardware and building supply stores. Usually the test requires you to ship or mail a sample of your water to a laboratory for analysis.

Fire Extinguishers

Home fire extinguishers are designed to put out small household fires. Every homeowner should keep at least one fire extinguisher in a handy location.

Types of Fires and Extinguishers

Household fire extinguishers apply agents that cool burning fuel, restrict or remove oxygen, or interfere with the chemical reaction so the fire cannot continue to burn. Deciding which extinguisher to place where depends on the type of fire most likely to occur in each area of the house:

- Class A fires, involving ordinary combustibles, such as wood, paper, cloth, upholstery, plastics, or similar materials, require either a water or dry chemical extinguisher.
- Class B fires, fueled by flammable liquids and gases, kitchen grease, paints, oil, kerosene, or gasoline, require the use of either a dry chemical, carbon dioxide, or halon extinguisher. (Never use water on this type of fire; instead of putting the fire out, the water may simply spread the fuel—and make the fire worse.)
- Class C fires, involving live electrical equipment or electric wires, require the use of a dry chemical, carbon dioxide, or halon extinguisher. If possible, cut off the electrical current at the source before using the extinguisher. Because of the electricity, never use water on a Class C fire.

Fire extinguishers are labeled using standard symbols and language explaining what kinds of fires the extinguisher has been designed to handle. *An ABC extinguisher will put out all three classes of fire.* When purchasing a fire extinguisher, discuss its intended use with the sales representative and let him or her guide your choice.

Routine Care

Check the pressure in your extinguisher each month (the pressure is usually readable on a dial near the top of the extinguisher). Most small hand-held extinguishers available for consumer use are disposed of after use. Larger extinguishers may be rechargeable. Read the manufacturer's literature carefully when purchasing a fire extinguisher.

Using a Fire Extinguisher

Placement and accessibility are important. Many of the smaller household models come with an attachment for wall mounting. Make sure all adults in the house know where the extinguisher is, can reach it in an emergency, and know how to operate it.

If you need to use a fire extinguisher, remember to stand 6 to 8 feet from the fire and follow the four steps of the acronym PASS:

P = PULL the pin. This unlocks the operating lever.
A = AIM low. Point the nozzle or hose at the base of the fire.
S = SQUEEZE the lever below the handle. This discharges the extinguisher.
S = SWEEP from side to side. Keep the extinguisher aimed at the base of the fire.

If you are unable to completely extinguish the fire immediately, leave the structure at once, make sure all occupants are safely away from the building, and call 911.

▶ **Fireplaces—See Chimneys, Fireplaces, and Wood-Burning Appliances**

Flooring

No one flooring material or floor covering is right for all situations. Different materials offer different aesthetic and practical features. Consequently, most homes incorporate several different types of flooring materials including resilient (vinyl, linoleum), wood, tile, marble, masonry, slate, and even concrete.

Many home designs use hard-surface flooring in high-traffic areas (such as entrances, kitchens, bathrooms, and utility rooms) because the hard surfaces are easier to keep clean and stand up well to the extra wear-and-tear. In particular, kitchen and bathroom floors take a beating. In addition to heavy foot traffic these floors are subjected to water and humidity day in and day out.

Routine Care

Routine floor care generally involves three tasks:

- keeping the floor clean
- preventing gouges, scrapes, or chips
- protecting the finish against stains and to minimize signs of aging due to wear and tear

Commercial cleaning products are available to clean and protect almost any floor finish. Remember when selecting cleaning products to choose products that will not dull or abrade the finish of your floor. Frequent light cleaning will protect a finish better than sporadic heavy cleaning.

Protect your floors against damage from foot traffic and furniture by using area rugs, furniture rests, protective mats at entrances, and by considering the type and placement of furnishings and decorations. When damage occurs (some stains, scrapes, and chips are inevitable over the lifetime of a floor) attend to it as quickly as possible. Many floor styles allow for replacement of individual tiles or sections with relative ease. Procrastination makes repair more difficult, however. If flooring has been chipped, gouged, deeply scratched or broken, dirt and moisture can quickly begin to penetrate the damaged section.

Resilient flooring, as its name implies, has a hard surface but gives slightly when you walk on it. Resilient flooring can be installed over most other materials if the subflooring is smooth, solid, and sound. Resilient flooring typically is made of vinyl, linoleum, asphalt, or rubber, and comes in a wide array of patterns and styles. To care for this kind of flooring, sweep, mop, and vacuum regularly to remove loose dirt. Wipe up spills immediately if possible. Remove dried spills with a damp sponge, cloth, or mop. Occasional damp mopping is also helpful. Dulled floors can be freshened by using a household floor cleaner as recommended by the floor manufacturer. Go as lightly as possible with the mop, cloth, or scrubber. Rinse the floor and let it dry. If the floor requires occasional polishing (some resilient flooring is designed never to need waxing) you will likely use a water emulsion wax. Apply new waxes and finishes only to clean, dry floors, and apply them sparingly. Let the new coating dry for about 30 minutes before allowing anyone to walk on it. Remove built-up polish or wax once or twice a year using a commercial remover. Dilute the remover, apply, rinse, let the floor dry, and apply a new coat of polish or wax.

Wood flooring is seeing a resurgence in popularity, especially given advances in protective finishes that allow for minimal care. Simulated wood flooring and combination products also are popular. Hardwood floors with a polyurethane finish need regular vacuuming or dry-mopping and an occasional wipe-down using a damp cloth or mop. Don't use too much water. Floors finished with anything other than polyurethane should not be cleaned with water: the water can cause the grain to rise and may cause eventual cracking from the expansion and shrinkage of wood that repeatedly absorbs water then dries out. Hardwood floors with other finishes may occasionally need waxing to keep up their shine. Use a liquid or paste "spirit" wax. If you use self-polishing waxes, make sure they are appropriate for use on hardwood floors. Buffing can be made easier by renting an electrical buffer. To minimize wax buildup, do not apply new wax right next to baseboards—little traffic occurs there to wear down the old wax.

Tile floors combine traditional good looks and endurance with great versatility. Unglazed and low-glaze tiles are less slippery and come in a kaleidoscope of colors, sizes, and shapes that won't fade or stain. Tile is also waterproof, unlike other materials, which are only water-resistant. Ceramic tile is almost maintenance-free. Wiping with a damp cloth or wet mopping will keep tile looking new. If grime builds up, occasional thorough cleaning using a detergent or ceramic tile cleaner will do the job. Use a stiff brush and a mild scouring powder on glazed tiles; unglazed tiles may be scrubbed or scraped.

The grout between tiles sometimes collects dirt or becomes stained. Use a fiber brush and mild cleanser to scrub away dirt; sealers are available to protect grout against staining.

Marble flooring can be extremely durable, depending on the quality of the installation, the thickness of the marble, and the amount of traffic over the floor. Use only a marble-cleaning solution that is appropriate for your particular floor. Marble stains easily and can be etched by harsh abrasives; it is prudent to invest in compatible sealing, polishing, and cleaning products as recommended by your builder or from a marble supply company.

Masonry or *slate floors* may be used in accent areas such as entryways. Slate floors can be sealed to make routine cleaning easier. After sealing, clean slate floors with a sponge or mop and a mild detergent solution.

Concrete flooring may be painted or unpainted. Unpainted floors can be cleaned using a solution of 4 to 6 tablespoons of washing soda to a gallon of hot water. Do not use soap. Before applying the cleaning solution, wet the floor with clear water, and rinse again after scrubbing with a stiff broom or brush. Sealing unpainted concrete floors can make them easier to keep clean. Follow manufacturer's instructions in applying the sealer and for cleaning after the sealer has been applied. Painted concrete floors can be cleaned using plain water or a mild soap or detergent solution. (For information on crack repair, see Paved Surfaces.)

Beneath Your Floors

No matter what type of flooring is installed, the subfloor and underlayment layers are the fundamental keys to maintaining a level, stable, quiet floor. The subfloor (the first layer of the floor) in older homes generally is made up of diagonal or straight planking. Newer homes usually have plywood subfloors. The next layer of the floor usually is some sort of underlayment. The underlayment should be well anchored with screws or nails driven directly through the subfloor into the floor joists for more stability. Construction adhesives often are used for extra holding strength.

As a wood floor ages it shrinks and warps, which may cause the floor to separate from the subfloor. Loose boards rubbing against nails or each other can cause squeaks in the floor. To repair a squeak from below, predrill up through the joist and into the subfloor, if possible right at the squeaky spot. Put a piece of masking tape on the drill bit to mark the proper depth so you don't drill up through the top of the finished floor. Then shoot a drywall or deck screw up into the floor. The screw should grab the plank and pull it down tight to the subfloor, eliminating the squeak.

If there isn't a joist in the area of the squeak, simply screw up through the subfloor into the plank. This method is not as effective, but it may help reduce or eliminate the squeaking. Unfortunately, it isn't always possible to get underneath a floor in finished areas of the house. In this case, locate the squeak and drill in a trim screw from above, at an angle into the location. Countersink the screwhead and fill any holes with wood putty. Then sand and finish the area where the repair has been made.

Foundations, Crawl Spaces, and Basements

Your home rests on a carefully prepared foundation. Preparation of the site for the foundation most likely included excavation, backfilling, leveling of the ground, and pouring or placement of a footing, usually made of concrete. (Just as your feet help balance and disperse your weight when you stand, the footing of a house helps balance and disperse the weight of the structure so that it does not shift or sink on stable ground.)

In some homes the rest of the foundation consists of a concrete slab and walls. Other homes are built on piers, with an open or partially open crawl space; others have a full basement. Foundation walls are built using concrete blocks, brick, stone, even treated wood. If you have a basement, the foundation walls also serve as the basement walls.

Partly above ground and partly below ground, foundation walls are subject to unique stresses relating to temperature changes and moisture. While the upper part of the wall expands and contracts (like all building materials) with daily and seasonal temperature changes, the underground part of the wall stays at a more constant temperature—and expands or contracts to a lesser degree. The difference in the rate of expansion and contraction in various parts of the wall causes pressures that can lead to cracking. The seams and joints where various components meet at the home's foundation present opportunities for moisture to enter, potentially aggravating this problem.

Modern construction techniques guard against water problems. You can best protect your foundation by ensuring that this system of dampproofing and drainage remains intact.

Routine Care

Routine care of your home's foundation basically boils down to observing changes in the foundation wall or basement, and taking swift action when repairs are needed. Whenever you are in the basement, take a moment to look at the walls and basement floor. By becoming familiar with how it usually looks, you are more likely to notice a change early on. When you walk around the house to check the condition of the siding and roof, also take a few minutes to examine the foundation walls and the ground next to the foundation.

Going inside, conduct another inspection of the entire foundation. Look for the following:

- significant cracks that allow moisture to seep through the wall or floor
- clogged weepholes in the lowest course of bricks (in a brick foundation)
- accumulated leaves or debris in window wells that can trap water
- poor grading as the ground outside approaches the foundation
- poor drainage under the foundation floor
- damaged cement or grout between stones or concrete blocks
- wet spots on walls or floor and other signs of excessive moisture, such as a musty, moldy, or mildewed smell

Condensation takes place wherever warm, moist air comes in contact with a colder surface. Moisture in the air can condense on a cold basement wall during the summer. Heavy condensation may even look as if moisture is seeping through the walls, pipes are leaking, or water is coming in through the windows. When you encounter moisture in a foundation, try to discern whether it is the result of condensation or a leak. To reduce condensation problems, close windows during damp, humid weather and open them during clear, dry weather. Keep in mind that new homes will experience more condensation as the concrete slab and walls will continue to cure for some time.

When inspecting a foundation wall for cracks or water damage, use a flashlight or worklight to ensure you have sufficient light. Check each wall from top to bottom along its entire length and check the foundation floor as it runs from each wall toward the center. Look for significant cracks (tiny, surface cracks may develop in a normal wall or floor as the concrete cures; such cracks generally do not cause structural or water problems). Note: Crawl spaces may be noticeably more damp than finished basements—but there should be no persistent standing water. Most crawl spaces are small, and if a moisture or vapor barrier has been installed in the crawl space it may be easily damaged by foot traffic. A visual check from the opening using a bright flashlight or floodlight should be sufficient to illuminate any serious problems.

Clogged weepholes in the lowest course of a brick foundation may become a source of water problems. If brick masonry forms all or a part of your foundation, check to be sure the weepholes have not been filled or become clogged by dirt. Similarly, window wells that accumulate leaves and debris cause problems because the moisture (or standing water) that collects there constantly presses against the most vulnerable points in a foundation wall.

Negative slope causes many water problems in basements and crawl spaces (see Landscaping and Yard Care). Negative slope can result from backfill settling, ground erosion, or changes in the soil from landscaping activities. Sometimes the solution is as simple as adding or removing soil to reinstate a positive slope away from the foundation. Add soil at the foundation only if a minimum of 6 inches of foundation wall will remain above ground level after backfilling.

Basements

Most basements are at least partially underground, and unfinished basements seldom have heat or air conditioning. These two conditions—combined with the frequent presence of clothes washers and dryers—heighten the likelihood of moisture problems.

Warm or hot water flowing from the washing machine into a utility sink in a cold basement creates water vapor that settles onto cold floors, walls, and windows and condenses. To reduce the likelihood of problems, extend the wastewater hose from the washing machine into the drain of the sink or into the nearest floor drain.

Poorly vented clothes dryers also can cause condensation problems in a basement. The exhaust hose should be free of holes or cracks and properly connected to the dryer. Check the seal where the coverplate that holds the hose in place penetrates the wall or window. During winter months, keep the vent free of snow. Blocked vents cause moisture-laden air to back up and escape into the basement.

Basement workshops that involve the use of steam or hot water can add to condensation problems. Install power fans in windows or through walls to adequately ventilate these areas.

Troubleshooting

To fill medium-sized cracks in foundation walls, first roughen the edge of the crack. Clean out all loose pieces of cement, mortar, or concrete using a wire brush or a thin blade. Wet the crack thoroughly, remove any standing water, then fill the crack with an appropriate patching cement. Allow a little extra cement for shrinkage. Just before the cement hardens, rub it with burlap or a similar material to give it a texture similar to that of the wall. (For a smooth surface, wet a trowel before going over the patch for the last time.)

To fill fine or hairline cracks, work a paste made from dry cement-base paint and water into the crack using a short, stiff bristle brush. If the original wall was painted you may be able to match the color by using a colored paint to form the base.

Large cracks generally can be filled using the same technique as medium-sized cracks, but you may need to cut into the concrete to ensure the patch will be secure. Cut a V-shaped groove to a depth about equal to the width of the crack at the surface. (See also Paved Surfaces.)

The best way to eliminate a leak will depend on local conditions that make each case different. Before making expensive repairs to correct wet-wall conditions, check to be sure your drainage system is functioning properly. Often correcting problems with grading (see Landscaping and Yard Care) or repairing or adjusting downspouts or gutters will help carry surface water away from foundation walls (see Gutters and Downspouts).

Installing a linear French drain is one way to control persistent problems with water drainage. Most homeowners will want to obtain expert help for this kind of project.

If you install a pump to remove water from your basement be sure the water that is pumped out drains well away from the house. For most home-owners, installation of a sump pump requires the services of a professional.

Tackle the job of repairing water damage to interior foundation walls only after the root problem has been correctly assessed and the root cause corrected. Scrape away loose material with a putty knife or a stiff-bristled whisk broom. Remove damaged cement or block down to a point where the remaining material is tightly bonded to the foundation wall.

▶ **Furnaces—See Heating Systems**

▶ **Ground Fault Circuit Interrupters (GFCIs)—See Circuit Breakers**

Gutters and Downspouts

Gutters and downspouts are critical elements of your home's self-defense strategy against the elements. They direct rainwater and melted snow from the roof to the ground and away from the house. Often when homeowners report problems with moisture and water seepage the first place a professional will check—and find problems—is with the gutters and downspouts.

Most gutters today are made of lightweight material—usually aluminum, vinyl, or plastic—and they are available in a variety of colors to complement the design and color of the home's exterior. Gutters fasten to the roof (and downspouts to the siding) using special clips and hangers that resist rust and minimize potential damage from the penetrations into roofing and siding material. Wherever various pieces of the gutter are joined together, sealants are applied to make the system watertight.

Routine Care

Regular maintenance of gutters and downspouts involves checking for storm damage, keeping them free of accumulated debris, decay, and rust, and tightening loose gutter hangers. Twice a year, check gutters to be sure leaves, twigs, or other debris blown up from the street have not clogged the gutters or downspout openings. Also, check the alignment of the gutters to make sure they are not bent or sagging. Gutters are installed with a slight slope that encourages water to flow toward the downspouts. Some bending is normal, especially at gutter seams, but serious bowing indicates a problem.

To check for proper drainage run water from a hose or bucket into the gutter. Look for puddling around the top of the downspout, slow-running water, or stoppages. Water puddling at the top of a downspout indicates a blockage somewhere inside the downspout. Shoot high-pressure water from the hose down into the downspout to force the blockage out. Slow-running water may indicate that heavy snow, ice loads, or ice dams have flattened out the slope that encourages water to run toward the downspout. If so the gutter hangers may also have been loosened—it's time to have a professional inspect the gutters and make repairs as necessary. Gutter installation is a task best left to professionals unless you are experienced with do-it-yourself projects.

Check the bottoms of all downspouts to be sure they are free of debris and that water exits at least 2 feet from the foundation of the house. Water rushing out of downspouts can easily cause water problems if it enters the ground too close to the house. The curved end pieces on downspouts direct water away from the house. If you desire, you can purchase extensions or perforated plastic hoses that carry water from downspouts to flower beds, lawns, or trees for irrigation.

Vinyl gutters never need to be repainted. Paint is optional for aluminum gutters. Gutters made from most other metals require a coat of rust-retardant paint, which may be applied at the same time the rest of the exterior is repainted.

A Note About Ice Dams

Clogged gutters can contribute to the formation of ice dams on a roof. The simplest preventive technique is to simply keep the gutters cleared and in good repair. However, in areas of the country that receive a lot of snow, and for gutters placed on high roofs, electric heating cables are available to eliminate this problem. Laid inside the gutters or fastened to the eave edge with special clips, the cables run on standard household current. Some gutter cables are equipped with sensors that turn the system on only when outdoor temperatures fall below 32° F. Others must be manually plugged in to turn them on. These cables are constructed to perform in outdoor environments while in contact with roofing materials. If installed and used properly they are safe and effective.

▶ Hardware—See chapter 6

Heating Systems

Every heating system has two operating cycles: the supply cycle and the return cycle. Depending on what type of heating system you have, the supply side of the system sends heated air, water, steam, or antifreeze from the heating plant to the various rooms of your home via a network of ducts or pipes. After the air, water, steam, or antifreeze gives off its heat, the return cycle recirculates it back to the heating plant. A control unit (almost always a thermostat) maintains a preset temperature by switching the heating plant on and off as needed.

In more complex zoned systems multiple control units regulate heat in different portions of the home. Heating may even be controlled according to the time of day. For example, you can set the control unit to keep room temperatures lower while you are out of the house and then warm up selected rooms shortly before you return. (For more information on zoned heating, see Home Automation.)

Natural gas, electricity, oil, or wood fuels the heating mechanism in most homes. All heating systems, regardless of the exact type, take advantage of the natural tendency of heat to move from warmer objects or spaces to cooler ones. This means a heat source (such as a burner, electric resistance element, or heat pump) can be coupled with a heating plant (usually a furnace or boiler). Consequently, there may be more than one source of heat in your home.

Routine Care of Furnaces

Most home furnaces work with forced air, hot water, steam, or radiant heating systems. Having your heating system professionally serviced each year just before the heating season helps ensure a comfortable, confident transition into colder weather. Schedule a complete cleaning and tune-up of your heating system. Combustion systems (those using natural gas or fuel oil) require a thorough cleaning to remove combustion byproducts. As seen in Figure 12 a gas- or oil-fired furnace has an exhaust pipe (also known as a flue or chimney) for the safe venting of exhaust gases. It is imperative that the exhaust gases have an unobstructed pathway to prevent deadly carbon monoxide gas from being released inside the home.

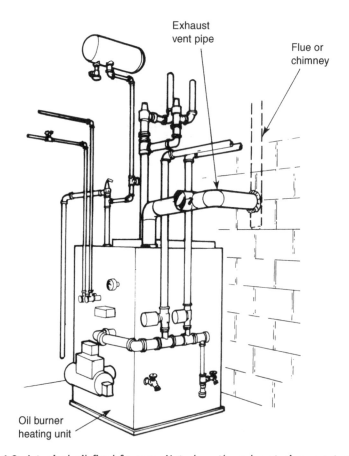

FIGURE 12 A typical oil-fired furnace. Note how the exhaust pipe penetrates the interior wall to join with the flue.

Equally important is to ensure an adequate, independent supply of air into the combustion chamber. Most heating systems use separate piping or ductwork to draw air from outside the home.

Although gas- and oil-fired systems normally require more maintenance, electric heat is not maintenance-free. Homes with electric heat should be serviced at least every two years. Have a service technician inspect the system, checking its components for efficiency, wear, and damage. Gas or electric furnaces need a professional tuning and cleaning at least every two years. Oil furnaces normally require inspection and servicing yearly.

The service technician also will check your fuel supply. Regulating the flow of fuel into the combustion chamber is a delicate matter; a slight adjustment can mean significant savings in fuel costs and a more comfortable home.

Homeowners are generally advised not to tamper with fuel tanks or supply lines; however, it is a good idea to keep grass and shrubbery trimmed away from exterior tanks and to visually inspect the tanks and lines from time to time. If you observe rust or damage, notify your service company. Homeowners whose heating systems use natural gas should become familiar with the exterior shut-off valve where your home's intake line connects to the main natural gas utility line (Figure 13). The supply line usually passes through a meter that tracks gas consumption. With a wrench this shutoff valve can be turned to stop all gas flow into the house. Each gas appliance in the home also has an individual shutoff valve.

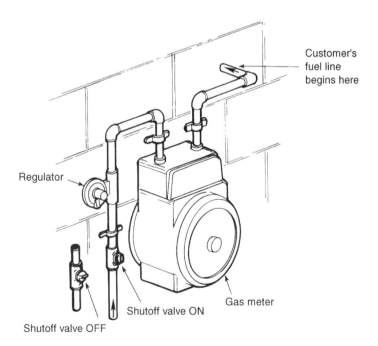

FIGURE 13 In an emergency the flow of natural gas to the home can be stopped by adjusting the cut-off valve. Never turn the gas flow back on: Call your gas utility company to perform this service.

Forced Air Systems

One of the easiest and most effective ways to keep forced air furnace systems running smoothly and efficiently is to change the air filters regularly. This prolongs the life of the furnace and improves the quality of your indoor air.

Clean or replace the air filter before turning on the furnace. Refer to the manufacturer's instruction manual for exact location, then remove and either replace or clean the filter, depending on the type. The manual will advise how often to clean or change it; but as a rule of thumb, plan on every 30 to 90 days. The arrows on the filter should point in the direction of the airflow.

One advantage of forced air systems is that the air circulating in the duct-work has already passed through the furnace filter, reducing levels of airborne dust and allergens. Changing the furnace filter monthly and having the entire system professionally cleaned on an annual or biannual basis helps keep forced air systems functioning in tiptop shape.

Forced air systems depend on supply and return vents (or registers) for the distribution of air (Figure 14). The vents may be equipped with louvers to open, close, or direct the flow of air into the room. Supply vents deliver heated air from the furnace to the various rooms of the house while cooler air is sent back to the furnace by way of cold air returns. Arrange furniture so that vents are unobstructed or hot and cold air pockets will form in the room, placing extra demand on the system. A blocked cold air return limits the amount of air getting back to the furnace, which could cause an imbalance in the airflow and add to the demand on the system.

Check vent covers to ensure they are wide open for maximum airflow. In the basement, locate supply pipes that branch off the furnace and feed each room. Each should have a damper control lever regulating the airflow to each room. Verify which you want opened or closed to maximize the benefits of zone heating. Note the direction the lever is pointing; opening the damper causes the lever to point in the same direction as the air flows in the pipe.

Hot Water and Steam Systems

Hot water and steam heating systems (sometimes called *piped systems)* rely on a series of pipes to carry the heated medium through the house. A pump transfers the heated water or steam from the boiler through the distribution pipes to radiators in each room. Today's radiators are most often quiet, efficient baseboard units that are part of a sealed system.

Baseboard radiator units use uninsulated, thin-walled tubing that allows the heat carried by the medium to radiate into the room. Vented covers placed over the tubing blend into the wall area, making baseboard units less noticeable.

Radiant Systems

Radiant floor systems can use conventional boilers. Hot water or steam travels to radiant zones (or circuits) throughout the home, eventually returning

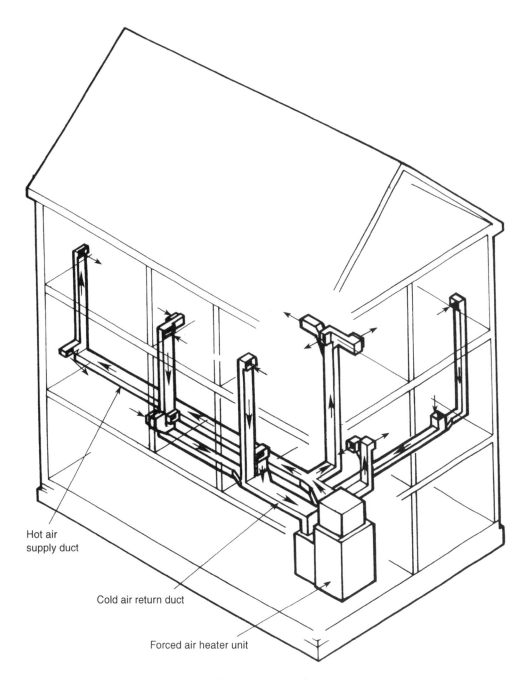

Hot air
supply duct

Cold air return duct

Forced air heater unit

FIGURE 14 The typical loop formed by the supply of warm air and return of cool air in a forced-air system.

to the boiler to be reheated. The circuits comprise lengths of hose that have been embedded in or installed beneath the flooring of each room. The durable hose can be used almost anywhere—in concrete, under tile, or attached to wooden subflooring. In some places radiant heating circuits are used in sidewalks and driveways to keep them free of snow and ice during the winter.

Heat Pumps

Two types of heat pumps are used in residential construction: ground source heat pumps and air-to-air heat exchangers. When used in conjunction with a water or earth storage system, heat pumps can save money and energy.

The beauty of heat-pump systems is that in hot weather they work in reverse to transfer heat away from the home, lessening the load on air-conditioning units and reducing cooling costs.

An air-to-air heat exchanger, normally part of a central air system, uses a system of chambers and coils to affect heat transference from air to coils and back to air again. Air-to-air heat exchangers also can be used to remove heat from indoor air, expelling it to the outside and lessening the load on air conditioners.

Follow the manufacturer's directions for changing a heat pump's operation from summer mode to winter mode. It's usually a simple procedure but important for proper operation.

Shutting Down the Heating System

Your heating system will need routine maintenance before it's shut off or changed over for the warm weather months. The kind of maintenance required depends on the type of system you have.

Conventional furnaces require only that the thermostat be set back. Most also have a separate main power switch, which when placed in the *off* position prevents the furnace from operating.

If the system also provides central air-conditioning, the power switch remains on while the thermostat is set back to a cooler temperature. A small switch on the thermostat changes the system from *heat* to *cool.*

Some furnaces continue to function throughout the year. Residential boiler heat systems are often equipped with an internal hot water heater (called a domestic hot water coil). These units produce hot water at a rate comparable to standalone hot water heaters even during the summer.

Troubleshooting

If your heating and air-conditioning system does not respond to the thermostat, check two items before calling a service technician. First, make sure the thermostat is set for the appropriate operation (heat or cool). Next, check the circuit breaker. If it's in the off position or has been tripped, reset it and try the thermostat again. If the circuit breaker is in the on position and the system still doesn't work, call in an expert.

Home Automation

Many new technologies in private homes come under the *home automation* label. Manufacturers of various labor-saving devices, appliances, and systems for the home have been promising the automated, or robotic, home of the future since the World's Fair days of the 1930s. Only recently, however, have technological advances become available at prices that make the "home of the future" a viable option.

Most home automation involves wiring and electrical connections; maintenance of the system requires little direct effort on the part of the homeowner, and changes to the system are best handled by professionals unless the homeowner is an expert.

Control Capabilities of Home Automation

New homes today frequently have whirlpool tubs, home offices, personal fax machines, home computers, and multiple phone lines. Kitchens are outfitted with microwave ovens, convection ovens, dishwashers, and coffeemakers among other time- and effort-saving appliances. Task lighting combines with area and accent lighting. A wide variety of security systems exist to meet almost any need. Your home's heating and air conditioning can also be automatically controlled for greater comfort and economy.

Control Units

Depending on what appliances and fixtures you wish to automate, control units (programmable devices that send signals to the appliances) can be either built into the wall or left in small tabletop boxes. Control units can turn devices on or off, or direct more delicate functions like temperature increases or decreases. A master control unit can be programmed to open or close draperies at various times throughout the day, or even water the gardens according to a set schedule. Some systems allow the homeowner to access and interact with the automation program while away by entering numeric codes over the phone.

Most home automation systems can work with the wiring normally found in new house construction. Ideally, the necessary electrical wires, phone wires, coaxial television cable, and (in some cases) fiber optic cables should be run throughout your house during construction. Special wiring can be added to existing homes, but the time and cost involved will be higher because the installation usually requires drilling holes into finished walls, floors, or ceilings, and making the necessary repairs to restore finishes after installation.

Security Systems

As Figure 15 shows, the home automation system can connect to your security system, phone system, and smoke and carbon monoxide detectors. These alert you to danger at hand and automatically dial the phone to summon police, fire, or health assistance.

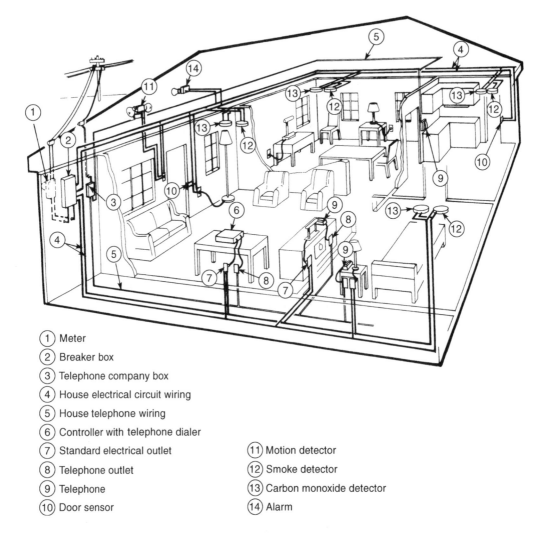

1. Meter
2. Breaker box
3. Telephone company box
4. House electrical circuit wiring
5. House telephone wiring
6. Controller with telephone dialer
7. Standard electrical outlet
8. Telephone outlet
9. Telephone
10. Door sensor
11. Motion detector
12. Smoke detector
13. Carbon monoxide detector
14. Alarm

FIGURE 15 Safety and security devices controlled by home automation systems are hard-wired to the home's power lines.

Closed circuit television (CCTV) systems also are now available that allow you to see who is at the door (or in any monitored room or area) from any television set in the home.

Heating and Cooling

Most new homes offer the convenience and versatility of a zoned heating and cooling system (Figure 16). A zoned system divides the house into zones in which the temperature can be controlled independently. By not heating or cooling rooms that are not usually used, you can gain potential capacity for the rest of the house and save money and energy.

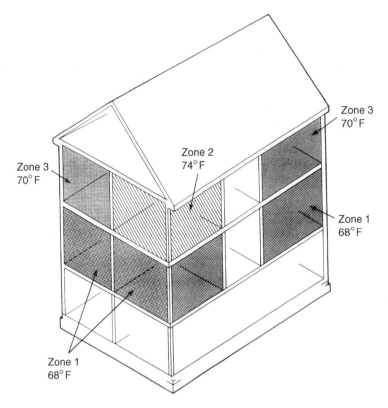

FIGURE 16 Example of a home divided into various temperature zones.

A home automation system takes zoned heating to another level, affording you the ability to automatically adjust temperatures throughout the house according to your schedule.

Electronic Interfacing

Electronic interfacing—for example, for a home office or a home theater—is an exciting part of home automation. Typically the electronic interface is built upon the lines run to the home for telephone service.

Star wiring, the preferred system today, runs bundles of cables from an interface box (where the phone company's cable enters the house) to each phone jack. Each bundle of wire forms an arm of the star coming from the box. If you are building a new home, ask to bundle video or data network lines in with the phone lines at this time. Even if you don't use the extra wiring right away, it's cost-efficient to have it all done at one time. More-advanced telephone features such as call waiting, hold, and conference calling usually require *twisted-pair* wire. Homeowners can also specify wiring for the following features:

- ISDN (Integrated Services Digital Network): High-speed ISDN technology permits two voice transmissions plus data transmission, all at the same time.

- Local Area Networks (LANs): Local Area Networks such as AppleTalk and Ethernet connect computer equipment via cable, carrying data within offices, homes, or campuses. LANs require separate cables that can be installed (bundled) with your phone wires.
- Partner panels: Partner panels allow a telecommunications system to link phone lines and be programmed to provide an array of features such as paging, conference calling, call transferring, door intercom, and on-hold music.
- Coaxial cable: Coaxial cable, or *coax*, is best known as the wire that brings cable television into your home and connects the VCR to the television set. Some cable television providers are branching out to provide Internet access through special modems and coax cable at a much higher speed than possible with phone lines.
- Interface controllers: Controllers transmit commands along the home's wiring to individual systems and appliances. You can network two or more computers, tie together home theater components, and share phone lines to send and receive voice calls, faxes, or data transfers. Controllers fit on a tabletop or can be built into a wall or installed as software on your computer.

In-line devices can now determine if an incoming call is a human voice, a fax, or another computer calling your computer and automatically direct the call to the appropriate device (Figure 17).

Interface devices allow you to extend the range of such items as television remote controls by generating an infrared (IR) light signal. These devices let you control a cable box, satellite dish, or VCR in the living room, for example, from your bedroom upstairs.

Home Security

Home security is a topic as old as the first bolted door. Although high-tech security systems are now available, much of home security still comes down to one basic principle: Make it hard enough to break in that potential thieves will bypass your home.

A well-maintained home and yard automatically enhances security because the appearance of care sends a message to potential thieves that your locks and other security features will likely be in good working order.

To discourage break-ins, check your home against the following list from time to time, and particularly when you are planning to be away from your home for an extended period:

- strong, working locks on windows and exterior doors
- gates on security fences closed and locked; doors to outbuildings closed and locked
- spare keys in the hands of a trusted neighbor or relative (not under the mat)
- front door outfitted with a peephole or working monitor

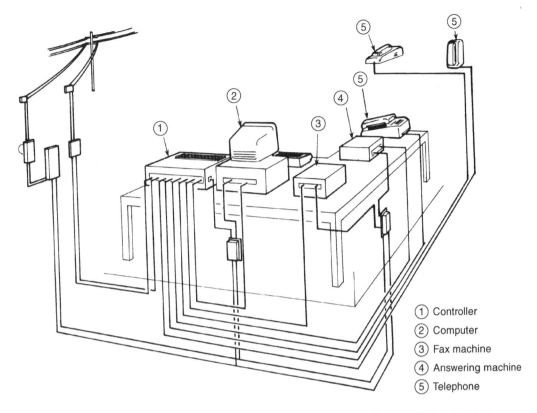

FIGURE 17 Making the most of phone line capabilities, a controller can distinguish between fax, voice, or data calls.

- exterior doors, including garage door, made of solid-core wood, steel, or fiberglass
- garage door opener codes secure (reset if unsure; don't use the factory-supplied code)
- garage door kept closed
- all windows closed
- exterior security lights working, out of easy reach
- fences, bushes, trees, other landscaping elements trimmed back from doors, windows
- ladders secured in garage or toolshed, or out of sight
- window blinds closed or shades drawn
- timers set
- detectors and alarm systems set
- mail and newspaper deliveries discontinued or pickup arranged

Landscaping and Yard Care

Proper care of your home's landscaping involves much more than just cutting the grass and trimming the hedges. Although those are important components in a well-kept yard, to maintain or improve the value of your investment you need to become aware of how grading, plantings, and maintenance activities affect your house and yard.

During summer months the shade from well-placed trees and bushes can reduce energy consumption required to cool indoor air. Healthy lawns prevent soil erosion and combine with the rest of the landscape to absorb noise. A well-tended yard provides a supportive and pleasant environment for your home, while poorly executed or tended landscaping can make exterior home maintenance more difficult and more expensive.

More specific information about trees and shrubs also appears in a separate section (see Trees and Shrubs).

The Landscaping Plan

Your home may come with well-established landscaping or with minimal plantings. Whether you are personalizing the yard of an existing home or creating the landscape for a new one, a good landscaping plan can help you increase the value and beauty of your home. Planning your landscaping according to how you want your grounds to look in ten years helps you maintain a long-range view. When developing your landscaping plan, consider the following:

- What trees, shrubs, plant, and grass varieties are commonly used in (or better, native to) your area?
- What spaces do you want to define for work, play, or as transitional areas?
- Where will you want shade? Privacy? Color? Walkways?
- Do you want spaces for specialty gardens (such as a butterfly garden or a garden with a pond)?

Make a sketch that includes the exact locations of the house, walks, walls, trees, shrubs, and other plantings. Note the locations of windows. Figure the space requirements of trees and shrubs at maturity—that way you won't have to move or thin out plantings later on. Consider whether the placement of plantings will block views or shut out light. And consider how plantings near the house may affect the grading next to the foundation.

Changes in Grade

Grade is a term contractors use to indicate the relative elevation of the ground surface at different points. When your house was built the contractor piled earth around the foundation to ensure that the ground surface at the foundation would be higher than the ground surface 3 feet away. The resulting grade allows rain and melting snow and ice to drain away from the house, reducing the likelihood of water damage.

Over time, fast-running water from storms or quick thaws can carry away surface soil, flattening out the grade. Because grading can be fairly subtle the changes may not be noticeable to you unless you periodically check the ground around the foundation. If topsoil has been washed away, water might be flowing toward your foundation instead of away from it (see also Foundations).

Digging and moving dirt tends to break up the soil and mix in air. As a result the backfill around a new foundation is typically fairly loose. Over time the dirt compresses from its own weight, the air slowly seeps out, and the surface elevation decreases. This process, called *settling*, can continue for years, and it is another important reason for you to periodically check the soil around your home's foundation. Settling may create bowl-shaped depressions that collect water. These depressions may be easily hidden by mulch or gravel, so be careful when checking for these low spots. Depressions may also develop where soil has been excavated and backfilled to lay or repair utility lines.

When you find problems with grading or settling, fill the areas with well-compacted topsoil to raise the elevation. Remember that the ground around your foundation should slope away from your house. A 1-inch fall per foot for at least 5 to 6 feet is preferred. Some experts recommend a slightly steeper slope, dropping 12 inches in the first 10 feet, tapering thereafter to a 2 percent slope. When planning garden beds near the house, do not disturb the earth next to the foundation; dig the beds several feet away to minimize the garden's impact on the foundation.

Erosion and the opposite problem, soil buildup, can occur naturally or reflect problems in landscape design. Water that erodes soil from one location will deposit that soil in another location. The soil deposits can create mounds that direct water toward the foundation of the house.

Buildups are usually easy to spot in the early spring as patches of bare dirt. Make sure to remove the buildup down to the original grade of the yard.

Landscaping schemes that elevate certain sections of the yard (such as flowerbeds) above grade can unwittingly contribute to basement water problems by channeling water toward the foundation. If you experience a water problem in the basement and have recently had landscaping work done, consider changes in elevation a possible cause.

Drainage swales are a special feature in some yards. A drainage swale is used to collect and direct rainwater, usually from several lots; the swale helps ensure that the ground in all the lots will drain properly, and helps prevent erosion and other problems. In some jurisdictions, water from four or five houses can collect in a sixth yard. Basically a ditch, the swale can nonetheless be very shallow, making it difficult for the homeowner to recognize. But the location of the swale is very important. If your lot contains a drainage swale, you will notice increased moisture or even open water running through the swale after a period of heavy rain. Because of potential drainage problems affecting adjoining properties, a drainage swale cannot be eliminated from an otherwise satisfactory lot. However, if you plan extensive landscaping or new construction that would affect the swale, your builder or remodeler may be able to relocate the swale or install an underground drainage line to carry the rainwater.

Lawn Care

In early spring (three to four weeks before trees begin to bud), start preparing your yard for the oncoming warm season. Spring feeding and weed prevention will show dividends throughout your lawn's growing season. Four or five feedings spread across the growing season at eight-week intervals also helps keep down weeds.

Most lawn fertilizers contain varying percentages of nitrogen, phosphorous, and potassium which improve grass color and density, enhance root growth, and promote general health and vigor. Many lawn fertilizers also contain insecticides and herbicides. Most of the time no other special treatment is required to control common insect pests and weeds such as broadleaf weeds or crabgrass.

Follow the fertilizer manufacturer's instructions for proper application. Most fertilizers should not be allowed to come in direct contact with flowers, plants, and flowering shrubs or trees. What fertilizer should you choose? The answer depends on the climate, soil acidity, available water, and type of grass in your yard. Consult with a qualified nursery professional for advice on the type(s) of fertilizers best suited to the grass, shrubs, and trees on your property.

Cut grass according to local weather conditions. When temperatures are high, set the lawnmower blade to cut the grass no shorter than 3 to 4 inches above ground level. Longer grass retains moisture better and protects the lawn's root system against heat shock. If cut too short during hot months, grass can burn and turn brown. In cooler climates many homeowners lower the blade to make a shorter cut in mid- to late-fall as temperatures start to drop. For lusher grass, also make it a habit to vary your mowing path. Cutting the grass at different angles helps disperse clippings, encouraging growth.

Twigs, stones, or other objects that strike a lawnmower blade will eventually dull it. A dull blade tears at the grass causing unnecessary damage. During the mowing season, inspect the blade periodically and sharpen the cutting edge as needed. Sharpening stones are available at hardware and home improvement stores. In last fall or winter, when you can go long periods between cuttings, take power mowers for an annual mechanical inspection and tune-up.

Watering

A portable sprinkler or built-in sprinkler system will provide a gentle, rain-like distribution of water over a broad entire area. Using a hose with a high-powered, rapid flow of water tends to cause puddling and runoff that flows into sewers, streets, and sidewalks, carrying away layers of topsoil and fertilizer along with it. The water fails to penetrate the soil and reach plants' root systems and the erosion also harms the yard. Always water early or late in the day. Water sitting on leaves, grass, and stems during peak sunshine hours intensifies the sun's rays and may burn leaves. Try to avoid sprinkling painted parts of the house when watering, as the sprinkling can reduce the life expectancy of the paint.

Insects in Your Yard

Many varieties of insects make their homes in our yards. Some insects benefit the landscaping, such as the bees that pollinate our plants. Other insects, such as bagworms, aphids, mites, beetles, hemlock, adelgid, and webworms, are potentially damaging to trees, shrubs, and grasses. Common signs of insect damage include:

- Airy bags of a silk-like material hanging from tree limbs
- Patches of grass loose enough to pull up easily with your hand
- Leaves with holes or chewed edges and interiors
- Normally green leaves that turn yellow or develop light green or yellow and white spots
- Sections of grass turning brown while surrounded by healthy green turf.

Home improvement and gardening stores stock a wide variety of insecticides and insect repellants. Many of these substances can be highly toxic to people or pets. And insecticides may wipe out beneficial insects along with the pests. Expert gardeners (and the experts at garden centers) often can suggest less toxic or even nonchemical solutions to repel or eliminate insects. Should you find yourself facing a serious infestation, however, consult with a professional exterminator who can safely apply the insecticide and advise you on how to ward off future problems.

Xeriscaping has increased in popularity in some parts of the United States. Xeriscaping is a water-conserving method of landscaping often used in arid or semi-arid climates. The basic principle is the use of plants, preferably native to the area, that require little water. This approach can be applied to solving problem areas of lawns and gardens in other parts of the country as well. For example, if you find that conditions in your yard simply won't sustain grasses or conventional gardens without continual (and expensive) treatments, consider planting alternative types of vegetation that will thrive with minimal care. Local nurseries or garden centers can usually provide information about alternatives appropriate to your area.

Lead in Paint, Water, and Soil

The dangers of lead, particularly to small children, have been increasingly publicized in recent years. High levels of lead in the bloodstream produce adverse effects on health and mental functioning. Since the late 1970s many steps have been taken to raise public consciousness about the dangers of lead and to remove lead from consumer products such as gasoline and exterior house paints. Many other products containing lead now carry labels advising consumers of the risks and proper handling to prevent lead absorption.

Pre-1978 construction may or may not contain lead. The ground surrounding older structures also may contain lead from fallen paint chips, particularly in the immediate area surrounding the foundation. Lead from older municipal or residential plumbing containing lead pipes or soldering can still get into drinking water.

Fortunately, homeowners can test for the presence of lead and, if it is found to be present, take steps to manage the problem. Inexpensive lead test kits are available in many hardware stores that detect lead on painted surfaces. Kits for testing lead in water and even in soil samples also are available. A useful free brochure, *Protecting Your Family from Lead in Your House,* is widely available at hardware and home supply centers.

If you find lead in your house, you can either have it removed or contain the hazard by sealing, or *encapsulating,* the lead with a special sealer. Lead removal is likely to be time-consuming, expensive, and—depending on the removal technique—potentially hazardous. Encapsulation techniques also require great care to ensure that the proper materials are precisely and thoroughly applied, completely containing the lead. Lead management is best handled by an experienced professional.

Both before and after encapsulation, homeowners are advised to keep dust levels under control by frequent mopping and washing with a phosphate detergent (5 to 8 percent solution). Besides ingesting lead by eating paint chips (the lead gives the paint a slightly sweet taste, which can be tempting for children), small children may get dust containing lead on their hands or clothes as they play, thus escalating their risk. Wet-mopping hard-surface floors each week and wiping down windowsills and baseboards with a phosphate detergent helps lower the risk. Wet mopping is more effective at removing dust than vacuuming, which can spread smaller dust particles rather than eliminate them.

If you find lead in your tap water, try to determine its source. Replace older plumbing that contains lead (don't forget to check for soldering that may contain lead), or install an efficient water filtering system to screen out the lead. Filters also can help if the lead originates further up the supply line (for example, in an older municipal system). When you use the tap for the first time in the morning, run the water for a few minutes before filling drink containers or cooking pots. Doing this flushes out the water that has sat in the pipes overnight and contains the highest concentrations of lead. Also, use only cold water for drinking, cooking, and preparing foods such as juices or formulas.

Lead in soil is extremely difficult and expensive to remove. Fortunately, the problem is likely to be confined to the area immediately next to the home's foundation and is most likely to be a problem only in homes built before 1960. Homeowners who discover lead in their soil can plant grass or other vegetation to cover the soil, plant small bushes and mulch close to exterior walls (to reduce the likelihood that children will play there) and restrict children from playing in crawl spaces under porches or homes. Do not allow small children to dig in the earth right next to the home's foundations, and when repainting the exterior of older homes be sure to collect and dispose of paint chips and scrapings properly in order to prevent further contamination.

Children's blood lead levels have dropped significantly over the last ten years. While excessive exposure to lead affects children across all social and economic strata, children in poor, inner-city families are disproportionately affected because lead-based paint hazards are more prevalent in older housing and the overall ambient level of environmental lead from all sources tends to be higher in inner cities.

According to data gathered by the Centers for Disease Control and Prevention, the risk for an elevated blood lead level was higher in non-Hispanic black children living in housing built before 1946, or built from 1946-1973, among children in low-income households who lived in housing built before 1948, and among children in areas with populations greater than 1 million people who live in housing built before 1948.

Masonry

Masonry surfaces in residential construction typically include brick, cement block, and various types of stone. Masonry is extremely durable, and most well-installed masonry can be expected to last for the lifetime of the home (see Figure 1). Routine care of masonry typically involves keeping it clean and free of stains and, occasionally, repairing the grout or mortar that holds the brick, block, or stone in place. Cosmetic care of masonry structures will be the same whether the masonry is structural or simply a veneer. Major problems with masonry generally relate to structural issues (such as settling of the house) or moisture penetration, which can have a number of causes. (For more information on moisture-related problems that affect masonry see Chimneys, Fireplaces, and Wood-Burning Appliances; also Foundations, Crawl Spaces, and Basements.)

Routine Care

The simplest way to clean masonry surfaces is simply to rinse them using a garden hose with the spray nozzle set for a hard stream. Start at the top of the structure and work your way down so that dirty water won't wash over cleaned areas. Masonry that has acquired a greenish stain may be harboring molds or mildew. To eliminate these types of stains, sponge or spray a chlorine-based cleaner or bleach directly on the stain. Rinse the area with plenty of clean water, reapply and rinse until the stain disappears.

Stains from grease, oil, paint, or other manmade products can be removed from masonry surfaces using a solution of muriatic acid. This chemical is available in hardware stores and is typically sold in a mild, 5 percent solution. Carefully read and follow the directions on the label. Use muriatic acid only in well-vented areas or outside, while wearing eye protection, rubber gloves, and long-sleeved shirts, long pants, and heavy shoes. Do not get muriatic acid on your skin. Situations requiring large-scale use of this product are often best referred to professionals.

Over time, weathering, acid rain, and corruption caused by molds and mildew can cause the mortar between joints to deteriorate and crumble as seen in Figure 18. Fortunately, mortar is relatively easy to replace using a technique called re-pointing.

FIGURE 18 A stone retaining wall in need of re-pointing to stabilize the mortar joints. Source: Original photograph by James Gerhart.

When you first notice crumbling mortar, act fast to prevent the problem from getting larger. Clean out the old mortar with a stiff bristle brush or broom. Use a strong stream of water to expel debris, brush again, re-wet, and allow to stand for 12 hours. Using a ready-to-mix cement patch material, mix up a medium to thin slurry and brush it carefully into the seams where the mortar used to be. Allow the slurry to dry completely, then wet the area thoroughly with water. Mix a fairly thick batch of ready-to-mix. You will know the mix is the correct consistency when a trowel face lightly covered with the mix can be turned upside down without the mix falling off.

Hold the supply of mortar close to the seam or joint you wish to re-point. Use a joint trowel to scrape the mortar into the seam, repeating until the seam is full. Use the flat bottom of the joint trowel to smooth the mortar. Begin working at a high point and proceed down the wall to prevent wet mortar from falling onto already-completed areas. Allow the mortar to dry completely.

▷ **Mold and Mildew—See Cleaning Interior and Exterior Surfaces**

Painting

Depending on the materials used to build your home, you may have virtually no surfaces that require painting—or you may be looking at a major project every five to ten years.

Exterior Surfaces

Paints formulated for exterior use are designed to take a beating and a well-executed paint job generally will last several years with mild to moderate touch ups. Some of the factors that can affect the durability of the paint are:

- Pollution: Even in relatively rural areas airborne pollution such as acid rain can erode the paint.
- Regional and local climate: Temperature ranges, variations in humidity, prevailing winds, levels of rainfall, and exposure to salt air or severe storms all affect the longevity of the paint.
- Siting and orientation of the home: Is the home atop an exposed hill or nestled in a sheltered valley? Broad wall surfaces exposed to blistering sun for much of the day will deteriorate faster.
- Technique: Even expensive high-quality paint will start to fail if it has simply been slapped over an unprepared or poorly prepared surface.

Even in mild climates, exposure to the elements and to seasonal changes in climate eventually wears down the paint on a home's exterior surfaces. Wet seasons and radical temperature changes can cause wood siding to expand and contract in a way that loosens paint. (Temperature fluctuations need not be seasonal. The same effect can be seen in dramatic form in areas such as the southwest and western United States, where year-round daytime high temperatures may differ from nighttime low temperatures by as much as 40° F).

In most of the continental United States weather fronts travel from west to east, subjecting west-facing walls to the harshest weather conditions. West-facing walls often need repainting first. Many new homes are deliberately placed to enhance energy efficiency and minimize damage from exposure to the elements. Landscaping also can be used to help shield new homes from wind, sun, and precipitation.

If your home is built close to a frequently traveled road you may already have noticed that more dirt and grime adheres to the exterior walls facing the road. All the dirt and dust that blows onto your home's siding contains sulfur particles, but the dirt that adheres to road-facing walls tends to include higher concentrations. When rain or snow comes into contact with sulphur it creates a mild form of sulfuric acid that deteriorates paint, brick, stone, and metal. Regular cleaning to keep exterior surfaces free of noticeable soot can help extend the life of the paint.

Interior Surfaces

How often the interior of your home will need touching up or repainting also depends on several factors, including your preferences. Some people repaint frequently simply to change the appearance of a room. Others repaint only when necessary. In either case, grease and carbon deposits from cooking and tobacco smoke cling to walls, floors, and ceilings and humidity from bathing, cooking, washing—even human respiration—eventually causes walls and ceilings to grow dingy. Indoor temperature and relative humidity affect paint longevity, and high traffic areas tend to get dirty faster. Although many interior paints are washable, each wash removes some paint along with the dirt. At some point you will need to renew the color.

Painting the House Yourself

Painting the house yourself can save money but doing a proper job takes time and considerable effort. Adequate planning, comparison shopping for materials and paint, a realistic budget and schedule, and thorough surface preparation are all-important elements of a satisfactory do-it-yourself house-painting project.

Selecting and Purchasing Paint

Glossy finishes are the easiest to clean, most durable, and moisture resistant. Low-gloss or flat paint (satin, eggshell, or lowluster) works well for large interior or exterior walls and ceilings. Semi-gloss and high-gloss paints work well for trim, kitchens, baths, laundry rooms, and other high-use, high-humidity areas. Alkyd paints are often used for high-humidity rooms such as bathrooms.

Paint colors now come in a wide range of hues, but almost any paint can be custom-mixed to your specifications. Keep in mind, however, that custom colors can be difficult to replicate exactly. Keeping a small quantity of leftover paint for touch-up work is not a bad idea if you have appropriate storage space, but the shelf life of paint does have limitations, so don't over-buy. If stored in an area that does not get too hot or too cold, an unopened can of paint may last for up to two years, and an opened can may last up to a year. Extremes of temperature (as occur in metal toolsheds and unconditioned spaces such as attics or garages) will shorten the life of the stored paint. Storing cans of paint and other flammable materials in the house is generally not recommended.

To estimate how much paint you will need, break each area to be painted into segments according to the type of paint to be used. Walls and ceilings are typically measured in square feet, while moldings and trim are measured in linear feet. Note the total square footage to be used with each paint. A dining room that measures 12 feet long, 8 feet high, and 9 feet wide might yield a list as follows:

Walls
336 square feet   Flat, medium blue, interior latex

Ceiling
108 square feet   Flat, white, latex ceiling paint

Trim
126 linear feet   White, eggshell interior latex

The cost of a gallon of paint varies with its quality and type. Less expensive paints often don't hold up to wear and tear as well as more expensive selections. In the long run, premium paints may yield the better bargain. Some dealers will provide quantity discounts if asked.

Some qualities to consider when evaluating paint include:

- hiding power
- adhesion (the paint's ability to stick to a surface)
- block resistance (the paint's ability to not stick to itself in areas like doors and their jambs)
- color acceptance (full, consistent color regardless of the method of application)
- touchup
- spatter resistance
- stain resistance
- stain removability
- burnish resistance (the paint's ability to avoid becoming shiny when rubbed or scrubbed)
- scrub resistance (the paint's ability to retain its color after being scrubbed)

Paint Types and Qualities

Oil-based paints have been used for generations as exterior house paints because of their good coverage qualities and excellent color retention. Oil-based paints dry to the highest gloss finish. For this reason, they are often used on front entrances or other areas the homeowner wishes to highlight. At one time, most oil-based paints contained lead, which made them more durable than other paints. Since the government mandated the removal of lead from paint, oil-based paints are no longer significantly more long-lasting than other paints.

Each coat of an oil-based paint requires approximately 48 hours to dry. If more than one coat will be required—for example, if you are changing the color of the house and want to be sure the new color is evenly applied—be sure to allow for sufficient drying time. Cleanup requires the use of solvents (such as mineral spirits) and drips need a steady hand to remedy.

Oil-based paints are relatively thick and heavy, so are best applied using china bristle or natural bristle brushes. Oil-based paints can be applied using a compressor, but they generally must be thinned according to the sprayer manufacturer's instructions. If you will apply oil-based paints using a compressor, wear gloves (to avoid having to scrub paint off your hands using chemical solvents) and follow instructions carefully and clean the compressor thoroughly after painting.

Latex paint has become very popular with homeowners and with professional painting contractors. Latex paint dries quickly, has excellent color retention, and resists peeling and blistering. The highest-quality latex paint today is 100 percent acrylic, a material that dries quickly and provides exceptional durability. Spills and tools used with latex paints usually can be cleaned up with water and (if necessary) a mild detergent. Polyester or nylon brushes provide the best results when used with latex semi-gloss or flat paint.

Alkyd paints feature a synthetic resin base and are a middle ground between oil-based and latex products. Alkyd paint takes longer to dry than latex but forms an exceptionally durable surface. Apply it to an absolutely dry surface to ensure proper bonding. *Urethane paints* adhere to most walls. *Epoxy paints* are usually reserved for tile, glass, and porcelain surfaces. Cleanup of all these types of paints requires solvents.

Stains allow the natural grain of wood to show through. Stains are available in latex and alkyd varieties. Latex stains retain their colors well and work best on water-resistant surfaces such as redwood and cedar. Alkyds penetrate wood to prevent cracking and are best suited for use on porous woods. Semitransparent penetrating stains alter the wood's natural color without obscuring its grain. Solid-color or opaque stains provide greater coverage, although some of the wood grain remains visible. This type of stain works well on lower grades of plywood or on blemished surfaces. Bleaching or weathering stains turn wood a silver-gray color without waiting for nature to weather the raw wood.

Stains vary in their degree of coverage. Clear coatings are available but can deteriorate quickly when applied to siding. If you want to protect the wood surface but retain a natural appearance, use a wood preservative that resists moisture, decay, fungus, insects, and warping.

Stains are among the easiest finishing products to use. Just brush them on and then wipe off any excess. Use a clean, dry brush to apply stain in the direction of the wood grain. Let it stand for a few minutes, then simply wipe it off with a clean rag. To achieve a darker hue, you can either let the stain stand longer before wiping or apply a second coat. If you've already gone too dark, you can rub off some of the pigment with a cloth moistened in the thinner recommended for the stain you're using. Stains can be applied using a compressor. (For more information about stains, see Decks and Platforms.)

Primers seal raw surfaces and provide a surface to which the final finish can better adhere. Situations that require a primer coat include painting new wood or wallboard, changing colors (especially from dark to light), and applying a flat paint over a glossy surface.

One purpose of the primer is to seal the surface pores in bare, damaged, or badly weathered wood. Priming helps keep the wood from absorbing too much paint. If the paint is absorbed too deeply it not only wastes paint, it also leaves the surface of the wood relatively unprotected and vulnerable to a condition called *bleeding through.*

If you are repainting you don't need to use a primer except where the wood has become exposed. If the surface is badly weathered, includes new materials or is bare wood, applying a primer coat before painting helps ensure smooth overall coverage and consistency of color after drying.

Primers are generally used with oil-based paints. Primer is not intended to hide the surface of the wood, only to seal its pores and provide a smooth paintable surface. Therefore, apply it very thinly, allowing the wood underneath to show through.

Surface Preparation

Plan to tackle large exterior maintenance projects such as painting or cleaning in weather that is warm but not too hot. Cleaners, solvents, primer, caulking, and paints are all easier to work with when temperatures are moderate and fairly constant. Indoor painting is, of course, less subject to the weather.

Homeowners who prefer to hire professionals for exterior and interior painting work can help their budgets by doing some of the prep work themselves. If you have already cleaned, scraped, and sanded the surfaces to be painted, the professionals will not need to spend much time on prep work—and you will save money.

Before painting indoors, move furniture into the center of the room and cover it and the bare floor with drop cloths, securing the edges of the drop cloths under furniture legs.

Outdoors an old bed sheet, blanket, or cloth or plastic drop cloth can protect areas such as:

- porches, decks, sidewalks, driveways, and railings
- landscaping such as plants, shrubs, and grass
- protruding architectural features such as bay or bow windows, entryways, and first-floor roof lines

Remove nails and picture hooks before you clean interior walls. Fill the holes as desired with spackling compound, or leave the holes in place if you intend to rehang the objects. When filling nail holes, overfill a bit to allow for shrinkage during drying. When the compound dies down sand it to the surface of the wall.

Remove any loose or peeling paint. Look for blisters, cracks, and peeled spots. These areas require scraping and sanding to smooth the surface and feather the edges. Feathering the edges where the painted surface meets the scraped surface makes them blend in with the surrounding area after you apply the new coat of paint.

For a top-quality paint job, wash down surfaces to be painted with a mixture of water and mild detergent. Washing removes grease and dirt that has adhered to the surface. Surfaces that have algae, fungus, or other biological invaders may need to be wiped or sprayed with a commercial mildew and fungicide or chlorine bleach solution. After cleaning rinse with clean water and allow the surface to dry completely.

Power washing can be a quick and efficient way to wash large exterior surfaces, particularly after scraping and sanding. Because power washers are so strong, however, inexperienced handlers may find it too easy to gouge and damage wood surfaces. After power washing, thorough rinsing and drying are important to ensure an adequate bond between the surface and the paint.

Lightly sand existing glossy paint with a fine-grit sandpaper before priming. Sanding roughens the surface, breaking the seal of the existing paint and promoting better adherence by the new paint.

Remove old paint from wood trim, doors, and the like using a chemical stripper or heat gun. Most chemical strippers require at least a two-step application procedure. Chemical strippers usually are brushed on, allowed to penetrate the paint, then removed by wiping off or gently scraping with a putty knife. Heat guns literally melt the paint to loosen it for scraping; be careful to keep the heat gun moving so as not to scorch the wood.

If you must remove paint from wood trim surfaces in an older building be sure to check whether the paint contains lead. If so, choose a method of removal that generates little dust and fumes, and be sure to properly dispose of the paint scrapings or residue (see Lead in Paint, Water, and Soil).

Establish a smooth surface for painting by filling nail or screw holes using a plastic, dough-type filler. Different mixtures are designed for filling holes in wood, wallboard, vinyl, and other materials. Tamp a small amount into the hole with your thumb. After the filler hardens use a fine sandpaper (such as 120 grit) to smooth the surface. Brush or blow away the dust from sanding before you paint.

For deeper or wider holes apply two or three layers of filler, letting each layer dry completely before filling further. Let your final layer overfill the void slightly to allow for the putty's tendency to shrink as it dries and to leave a base for sanding.

Use masking tape and newspaper or drop cloths as needed to shield windows, trim, or other areas from the paint. Taking the time to do this properly can save you hours of tedious cleanup. Be sure to remove the tape while the paint is still tacky; otherwise the tape may be difficult to remove and you risk leaving a ragged edge where the tape meets the painted surface.

Tools

Take some time to assemble the tools, equipment, and accessories you will need to tackle your painting job. (You will find more information about tools in chapter 6.) Select high quality tools that will help you minimize the work. This is not the place to skimp in your budget.

You will likely need the following tools and materials:

- brushes of various styles and sizes appropriate to the paint and the job
- claw hammer
- drop cloth(s) or newspapers
- edgers
- face mask or respirator
- ladders, possibly also scaffolding
- masking tape
- paint and (as appropriate) primer
- paint pan(s) and liners

- putty knife
- rags
- rollers and roller covers
- roller handle extension
- safety goggles
- sandpaper (medium and fine grit)
- scrapers
- spackling, putty, or specialized filler material
- sponges
- work boots
- work gloves

Your safety and comfort should be as primary a consideration as the quality of the paint job. Dust, wood chips, or bits of paint lodged in an eye at best cause inconvenience, and at worst serious injury. Some paints and paint thinners contain strong chemicals whose fumes can be damaging; masks and respirators are used to protect your health. And sturdy work gloves and boots help safeguard your hands and feet against injury. When purchasing or gathering tools for your painting project, keep safety-related items at the top of the list.

Technique

Compression painting is faster than painting with brushes and rollers. However, there are some drawbacks, including the following:

- When using a sprayer, much more masking will be required. Since the paint is actually airborne, it will drift with the air currents. It is also very easy to overspray.
- Use of a painter's mask is very important with compression painting to prevent breathing airborne paint.
- Although the paint is dispensed quickly, the sprayer must be kept moving at all times to avoid buildups and drips. It is not easy to produce even coverage.
- The nozzle of the sprayer must be kept 4 to 6 inches away from the surface; holding the nozzle at varying distances can lead to uneven coverage.
- Cleanup can be more time-consuming when you use compression sprayers.

Small objects such as removable trim pieces can be sprayed inside an improvised painting booth made from cardboard and clear plastic.

To paint using brushes, begin applying the paint with short strokes, laying down paint in both directions. (For wood surfaces, direct the paint across the wood grain.) Resist the temptation to bear down too hard on the bristles; instead, let the paint flow off the brush instead of squeezing it off. Finish painting with longer, sweeping strokes in one direction only. (For wood surfaces, this layer goes on with the wood grain.) For a professional-looking finish, sand lightly between each coat of paint you apply. Any wood finish applied in successive coats will look better and last longer if the surface is lightly abraded between coats. Use just enough pressure to let the tips of the bristles contact the surface in order to level the paint. This two-step technique ensures complete coverage of the surface and is useful for applying varnishes.

To cut-in wall surfaces around woodwork, use tape to mask all adjacent wood surfaces, butting the tape against the wall. Then you can work your brush all the way into the corners without worrying about spilling over onto the wood.

Use rollers to paint large areas. To achieve complete, uniform coverage, load the roller with paint and begin applying it in with smooth, even pressure. Gradually increase the pressure to squeeze out more paint as you go. Cross-roll with opposing strokes to level the paint and to fill in between your initial strokes.

Painting walls may be the easiest way to redecorate, but it takes a patient, steady hand when painting around fixtures and cabinets. Sufficiently masking these areas not only speeds the process, it decreases or eliminates much of your clean-up time.

▷ **Paneling—See Walls**

Paved Surfaces

The majority of residential walkways and driveways are either asphalt or concrete, and many patios and steps are made of concrete. While driveways, walks, patios and steps are designed to withstand the elements and heavy-duty wear and tear, they do require some maintenance. Cared for properly, a concrete patio or walkway may last for more than 20 years; an asphalt driveway, about 10 years.

Routine Care

Routine care of most paved surfaces basically involves the following:

- sweeping surfaces clean from time to time (particularly if wet leaves have accumulated on the pavement)
- removing snow and ice after winter storms
- patching cracks in a timely manner

Removing Snow and Ice

Prompt removal of snow from paved surfaces is important for several reasons:

- Community ordinances may require homeowners to remove snow from public areas within a specified amount of time (usually 12 to 24 hours).

- A person who slips and falls on a snow-covered sidewalk outside your home can file a suit against you.
- Prompt removal of snow helps reduce ice formation, and ice is much harder both to walk on and to remove.
- Finally, removing the snow protects paved surfaces from damage.

Shoveling snow is a much more strenuous activity than most of us think. Pacing yourself, taking frequent breaks, and lifting smaller, more manageable loads lessens your risk of muscle strain, back injury, and heart attack. Lift with your legs, not with your back—and use the right shovel.

Figure 19 shows several types of shovels, including an ergonomic design that puts less strain on the back. Another option is to use what used to be called a coal shovel. The heads of coal shovels have wide, deep blades that give them a large capacity. The plastic head decreases the weight of the shovel and provides a slippery surface that snow doesn't stick to. The wide blade glides easily under snow and ice, making it easier to get down to the pavement.

The best way to shovel snow is to plow the snow from the pavement instead of lifting and throwing it. If the snow is wet and heavy, plow the snow across the sidewalk instead of lengthwise. Tilt the handle forward at the end of a pass and use your foot to nudge the snow off the head onto the curbside. With this plowing technique the shovel is less likely to gouge the pavement underneath the snow.

When sleet or freezing rain deposits a layer of ice on your pavements, flat-headed tools called chippers or scrapers offer thinly ground edges that can break up the ice and get between the ice and the pavement. Holding the handle of the tool, lift the blade of the chipper 6 to 12 inches above the surface of the ice. Let the handle slide through your hands, letting gravity control the

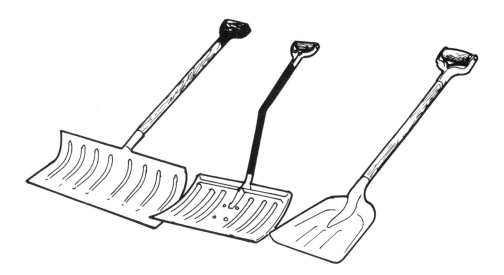

FIGURE 19 A traditional snow shovel, an ergonomically designed snow shovel, and a deep-faced coal shovel offer homeowners a choice in snow-removal equipment.

impact of the blade against the ice. Repeat this action several times until the ice cracks.

If you don't have a chipper, try turning a shovel to use the corner or point of the blade. Do not strike the ice; instead, apply pressure to the point by leaning on the handle. Homeowners living in areas with long or severe winters who have long or wide driveways or corner properties that are surrounded by sidewalks may want to invest in a snowblower (see chapter 6).

Removing ice from sidewalks and driveways can be a far more difficult task than removing snow. Ice also presents a greater safety hazard, so prompt removal is even more important.

Rock salt will melt ice but also tends to react with concrete, deteriorating and pitting the pavement and enlarging cracks. If inadvertently spilled onto grassy areas, salt can burn and kill the grass. And, as the ice melts, the salt and water tend to form a brine that can damage shoes, slacks, and carpets.

Chemical ice melters tend to cost more than rock salt and can leave stains on pavement. Chemical ice melters should be used as a last resort on thick layers of ice. Try using cat litter or sand instead of chemical de-icers for traction on icy sidewalks, steps, and driveways. Litter and sand won't harm plants, poison runoff water, or erode concrete.

Chemical deposits leave white stains on pavement. It is advisable to clean and check your driveway and walks each spring to assess damage from chemical deposits, making repairs while the job is still small. To rinse concrete and asphalt free of chemical residues, spray the area with a continuous stream from your garden hose. Set the nozzle of the hose for a high-pressure stream or use a power washer. Direct the flow of water toward a drain or sewer and keep the water from flowing onto your grass, flowerbeds, or bushes. After spraying scrub affected areas with a stiff-bristle broom to loosen the chemical residue from the surface, then rinse again. Repeat the process until all signs of the stain are gone.

Cracked, pitted, or spalled (eroded) pavement in walks or drives should be patched as soon as possible to prevent greater damage. While you needn't fill every tiny crack, be sure to take care of cracks 1/4 inch or larger in size. Many different fillers are on the market. Read manufacturer's instructions on product packaging before you make your purchase. Some products are designed to fill shallow cracks, others are all-purpose fillers, and some have restrictions on the width of the crack being filled. Ready-to-mix products are available for patching larger areas. Generally all you have to do is add water and mix. Follow the manufacturer's directions carefully; the amount of water to add depends on the application.

Sealing Asphalt

Blacktop or asphalt paving is a mixture of small pieces of stone and sand held together with asphalt cement. Properly installed asphalt remains pliable for a long period of time, which gives the pavement a certain amount of crack resistance. However, asphalt can become brittle and develop cracks as it dete-

---

Safety Note: Wear long-sleeved shirts and long pants, goggles, a face mask, and gloves when handling concrete mix. Concrete is highly caustic; the dust can irritate your eyes and lung tissue, and once activated by water the concrete mix can cause severe burns to exposed skin.

---

riorates from exposure to sunlight and oxygen. Asphalt pavements may be sealed at some point during the first year after installation. (Sealers are not applied immediately after installation because the concrete mix in the pavement requires time to fully cure.) Sealers prevent damaging air and sunlight from reaching the asphalt cement.

Do not be too anxious to reseal asphalt pavements too frequently. Sealers are finish coats, like paint; applying too much will result in cracking and peeling. Reseal the driveway only after you can clearly see that the old sealer is wearing down. As the sealer wears away, the color of the surface will begin to lighten as the aggregate in the asphalt mix begins to show through. When you notice large areas of this color change, plan to reseal the pavement.

Repairing Asphalt

When potholes and large cracks occur in an asphalt driveway, the entire path or driveway need not be replaced. Filling in faults, shoring up weak points, and properly sealing the surface can restore the pavement to serviceable condition. Different products are available for potholes and cracks of different sizes.

When repairing a crack, remove all loose debris. A masonry chisel and mallet can extract stubborn chunks of broken asphalt. Make sure you wear safety glasses. After loose debris is removed, clean the crack well. The patch will adhere to the crack properly only if free from all foreign material. Sweep with a broom, then wash out with a garden hose. If it's likely the crack contains oil, use a stiff brush and detergent to scrub it clean. Allow washed surfaces to dry completely.

Cracks wider than 1/2 inch should be filled using an asphalt cold patch, available in bags or cans. This material is highly compressible; pour it into the crack and tamp down well. Repeat this process until the patch is even with the surrounding surface levels.

Potholes are familiar to all of us. When these relatively deep gouges appear, additional repair work is needed. Dig out loose material and dirt until a solid base is reached. If the edges of the hole are soft and crumbling, use a shovel to cut back to firmer material. Clean away all dirt and foreign debris, then fill the hole to within four inches of the surface with well-tamped gravel. Next, apply a layer of cold patch material less than 2 inches thick.

Tamp the cold patch thoroughly until fully compacted and repeat until the cold patch is within an inch of the surface. The final layer of cold patch should extend just above the surrounding surface. Tamp firmly or place boards over the patch and drive over it several times to compact this layer.

Allow the repair to cure for 12 to 36 hours before driving on it and 2 to 5 more days before sealing the entire driveway.

Repairing Concrete

Concrete is a combination of aggregate and sand mixed with portland cement and water. When correctly mixed, poured, and finished, the water in the concrete slowly evaporates. The longer it takes for the moisture to leave, the stronger the remaining concrete becomes. Well-cured concrete is usually hard and durable, damaged only by tree and plant roots growing underneath it or the heavy use of rock salt during winter.

Treat and fill small cracks in concrete with cement crack filler. Make sure the edges of the crack are firm; if not, knock them off using a hammer and chisel. Clean the crack with a broom, then wash with a strong stream of water from the hose and let dry. Fill in the crack to a level just above the surrounding surface level; this allows for shrinkage.

Follow the directions on the package for drying time. If the crack repair remains slightly higher than the surrounding surface level, don't try to level it off by chipping away at it. Removing the top seal will weaken the patch, causing it to crumble. Cement crack filler comes in varieties designed for specific applications; choose one for the size of the crack you are filling. Powdered form and squeeze bottles are available, or use a regular cement mix.

Larger cracks, spalling, and delaminations all are treatable with ready-to-mix products. Clean the affected area as described. Mix a thin, watery slurry of the ready-to-mix product and brush it liberally over the entire area. This forms a liner coat that will help the patch stick. Because slurry has a high percentage of water it takes quite a while to dry, but leave time for it to dry completely before proceeding.

Once the slurry coat is dry, clean it again to remove any dirt or dust that may have settled during drying. Thoroughly wet the area to be patched and allow it to stand wet up to 12 hours before proceeding. Remove any standing water or any debris. Follow package directions to mix a batch of ready-to-mix material, then pour it into the area and use a trowel to spread it evenly. Do not apply more than a 2-inch layer of ready-to-mix at a time. Allow the first layer to dry completely before applying the second. Repeat this process until you have filled the area to just slightly above the surrounding surface level and let dry completely.

Concrete surfaces that crumble, leaving the concrete just below the surface in good shape, can be repaired with thin overlays. For best results, use a fully bonded overlay. This involves placing a 1- to 2-inch layer of concrete into the affected area that will physically and chemically bond to the existing concrete.

The proportion of cement in the concrete mixture and the size of the aggregate are critical. Each cubic yard of concrete mixed must have a minimum of 600 pounds of cement. The maximum diameter of any stone used as aggregate must not exceed one-third the thickness of the overlay. If your overlay is very thin, eliminate the aggregate from the mixture.

Prepare the area for patching by cleaning the entire surface and chipping away existing loose material to ensure solid concrete below. Rinse the surface to remove grease and dirt, then keep it wet for 12 hours before applying the concrete to improve bonding. Apply a slightly thick slurry mixture the consistency of a quality latex paint. Instead of a liner coat, the slurry is applied in a 1/16-inch film just before the concrete mixture is poured. It is ideal if two people handle this task; one lays down the slurry just ahead of the concrete mixture.

It is crucial that the slurry does not dry before being covered with the concrete overlay. Apply a liquid curing compound immediately after finishing each section. Cover the overlay with plastic to eliminate rapid water loss. For best results, do this type of repair in cool, overcast weather.

Efflorescence is a white, powdery deposit that may appear on concrete surfaces as anything from a light haze to a heavy spreading pattern called blooming. Efflorescence results from water traveling through the surfacing material. When the water evaporates from the surface the salts are left behind causing the telltale white stains. Efflorescence can occur even after a surface has been sealed.

Not all white or hazy stains are efflorescence. Hard-water deposits from sprinklers or rain runoff can cause similar stains, but these will appear on the surface of the sealer, not underneath. If the stain wipes off on a damp finger, it probably is not efflorescence.

Over time, given repeated cycles of wetness and dryness, the powdery efflorescence can change to a crystalline structure that adheres tightly to the surface. Once crystallized, the stained areas must be pre-treated with special chemicals, as the stain will no longer respond to a basic cleaning treatment.

Plumbing

Many plumbing problems can be avoided with a little preventive maintenance. When problems arise, prompt attention to them is usually the best way to keep repair costs down.

Features of your plumbing system that you should become familiar with include the following:

- septic system
- intake valves
- pipes, traps, and cleanouts
- faucets
- toilets

Your home may be served by a municipal sewer system or use a septic system to handle waste. As with your water system, if your home is connected to a municipal system you will typically have responsibility for backups or plumbing problems up to the street, and the municipal authorities will handle problems from that point onward.

If your home has a septic tank, know where the tank has been placed, as well as the boundaries of its drainage field. Check the tank once a year to monitor how quickly it is filling with solid wastes. Most tanks of normal size require cleaning every two years or so—but if you use a garbage disposal the tank may need cleaning slightly more often. When the depth of solids and scummy material reaches more than a third that of the liquid in the tank, it is time to have it cleaned by a professional service company that can dispose of the contents in compliance with local health codes.

Every adult in your house should be able to locate the water intake valves for your plumbing system (also called shutoff valves, or stop valves). In the event of an emergency, or if you need to make minor repairs, you will want to know where they are. One easy way to do this is to label each one with a shipping or luggage tag. Don't wait until an emergency to find the intake valve; mark their locations and test their operation from time to time. As shown in Figure 20 the master intake valve usually is located on the main intake pipe shortly after it leaves the meter.

The intake valve can be designed several ways. Usually, simply turning the handle will stop all water from flowing past that point. When you close the valve and the water stops flowing, open a faucet (in a sink or bathtub) to drain the pressurized water already in the system. Doing this before you start to repair a leak or replace a fixture will prevent accidental spraying and make the job easier.

All of your plumbing fixtures (except the toilet) empty into traps (those funny, curved sections of pipe). Toilets are trapped internally and drain directly into the main drain.

One or more cleanouts in the main drain allow access for clearing clogged lines. Traps serve the same functions for fixture drains. In an efficiently designed home most fixtures will cluster near a common wet wall. The wet wall is usually a few inches thicker than other walls to accommodate the 3- or 4-inch diameter stack used in residential construction. Hot and cold supply lines may also be located in the wet wall. To identify your wet wall, look for where the stack emerges from your roof.

A Note About Exterior Faucets: Water faucets located outside or in unheated garages or basement areas are vulnerable to freezing and splitting. Cold temperatures can easily cause water inside a faucet to freeze, expand, and split the pipe or the faucet itself, causing water damage to the exterior and sometimes the interior of the home. Before freezing weather arrives, turn off the water source to exterior faucets by adjusting the shut-off valve at the faucet. (Remove the garden hose for storage—do not leave it attached to the faucet.) Open the faucet to drain out any standing water. Leave it open as a safety precaution. Some stores and catalogs promote the use of faucet covers or jackets. These are fine as added protection, but are no substitute for taking the faucet off-line and draining it.

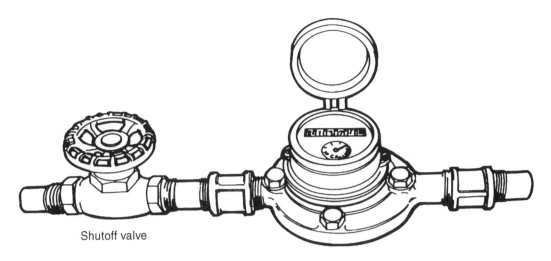

Shutoff valve

FIGURE 20 Water flow to the entire house can be controlled with the intake (or shutoff) valve.

Think of the main stack as a two-way chimney: water and wastes go down, gases go up. If you install new plumbing fixtures, be sure the lines are properly vented. Strangle a drain's air supply and you risk creating a siphoning effect that sucks water out of the trap, breaking the seal that protects you against gas backups.

The life expectancy of your faucets depends on the initial quality of the faucet and on the type of finish. Generally high-quality faucets can be expected to outlast lower-quality faucets by several years, and a chrome finish will last longer than brass or enamel.

The new low-flush models of toilets use far less water than previous models. Preventing overflows or clogs in toilets (old or new) generally means keeping the working parts clean and avoiding flushing anything that could catch in a pipe. Never flush materials such as hair, grease, garbage, lint, diapers, sanitary pads, or rubbish. Caution: Read the labels of cleaning products carefully and do not mix products. Some bathroom and toilet cleaners produce hazardous, even lethal fumes if mixed with household bleach or other cleaning products.

Routine Care

Routine maintenance should include the periodic use of a drain cleaner to ensure the proper flow of water through the system. Many commercial drain openers use a caustic, or mildly acid, solution to bore a hole through the clog and open a route for the water to pass. Unfortunately, that doesn't clear the clog clinging to the side of the pipe.

A few commercial products contain bacteria specifically cultured for use in drainpipes. When these products are used regularly (at least monthly) the bacteria continually eat away at the material attached to the walls of the pipes, keeping them clear.

Some simple natural remedies can also keep your drains flowing. (The same remedies often will work for a clogged toilet.) Pour a large pan of boiling water down the drain weekly to maintain an open drain. To unclog drains, pour in 1/2 cup baking soda followed by 1/2 cup vinegar. Cover and wait several minutes, then flush with boiling water.

When pipes that drain from tubs, sinks, or showers become clogged, you can try chemical drain cleaners or use a plunger. Plug overflow outlets, if any, with a rag. If you are working on a double sink, be sure to close the other drain.

A plumber's snake is a good second-level solution. (Snakes can be rented or purchased.) Turn the handle of the snake in the same direction when removing it as you did when inserting it so that the material "caught" by the snake does not come loose as you draw it out. If a drain remains partly clogged after plunging or snaking, pour boiling water (140° F for plastic pipes) into it, or open the trap under the fixture. Put a pail under the trap to catch the water.

Caring for Faucets

Protect the finish on your faucets by using appropriate nonabrasive cleaners and by wiping up splashes promptly using a soft cloth. With normal use, faucets will occasionally need attention to stop drips or leaks, or to have their aerators cleaned (most often in kitchen and bathroom sinks). Every 3 to 4 months (possibly more often, depending on the condition of the water) unscrew the aerator from the mouth of the faucet; remove any deposits; remove and rinse the screens and washers; replace the screens and washers in their original positions; and screw the aerator back on the faucet.

Preventing Leaks

Simple preventive maintenance can help you avoid the causes of many leaks and protect your home. Drippy faucets often can be fixed by replacing old washers or cartridges (on faucets with single controls for hot and cold water). Turn off the water at the intake valve closest to the faucet before you begin work on the faucet!

Apparent leaks near toilets sometimes prove to be only condensation forming on the outside of the tank and dripping to the floor. If water leaks into the toilet bowl from the overflow pipe, bend the float rod slightly so the tank will stop refilling at a lower level. Other sources of trickling water may be a washer at the intake valve that needs replacing, or faulty alignment between the ball valve and the flushing handle.

Leaks at joints in copper or plastic pipes are best repaired by a professional plumber.

A Note About Exterior Faucets: Water faucets located outside or in unheated garages or basement areas are vulnerable to freezing and splitting. Cold temperatures can easily cause water inside a faucet to freeze, expand, and split the pipe or the faucet itself, causing water damage to the exterior and sometimes the interior of the home. Before freezing weather arrives, turn off the water source to exterior faucets by adjusting the shut-off valve at the faucet. (Remove the garden hose for storage—do not leave it attached to the faucet.) Open the faucet to drain out any standing water. Leave it open as a safety precaution. Some stores and catalogs promote the use of faucet covers or jackets. These are fine as added protection, but are no substitute for taking the faucet off-line and draining it.

Noisy pipes may result from worn washers, loose parts in a faucet, or steam in a hot water pipe. Noise may be accompanied by vibration, which can eventually shake loose fittings, causing leaks.

Insulating Pipes

Insulation keeps coldwater pipes from sweating in warm weather and hot-water pipes from freezing in winter. Insulated pipes retain heat better, so the water in the pipes stays hot longer.

Pipe insulation comes in a variety of forms. A liquid or paste form of asphalt containing finely ground cork offers the most protection for coldwater pipes. Brush on one or more applications to build up an appropriate thickness. Fiberglass insulation with foil backing is effective and inexpensive. Cut it into strips for an easy wrap-around installation.

Self-stick tapes with special insulating qualities are effective for both hot- and coldwater pipes. One version, a puttylike tape, spirals around pipes, easily forming around fittings.

The most popular form of pipe insulation is a jacket made from plastic foam, wool felt, or fiberglass. These pipe jackets come in 3-foot lengths and feature a split that easily slips over straight pipe runs.

If you will be away from home for any length of time during the winter months, set the thermostats at a minimum of 68° F to help ensure that pipes and faucets don't freeze while you're gone.

If you expect a spell of extremely cold weather, turn water faucets on to make sure pipes haven't already frozen. Leave a trickle of water moving through the pipes. Running water won't freeze, and the cost of the additional water pales in comparison with the repair costs for burst pipes.

Roofs

Performing routine inspections and maintenance of your roof may prevent or delay costly repairs or replacement. Some roof maintenance tasks require a pro-

What if the Pipes Freeze? If exposed pipes do freeze, try a hair dryer set on its highest setting to blow hot air over the frozen pipe. Direct the hot air parallel to the run of the pipe, not square on to a small section of pipe. Also, open all faucets connected to the lines so that steam can escape if any forms during thawing. Never use blowtorches or electrical devices such as heating pads, which could start a fire or electrical short. Have patience: Thawing a pipe too quickly may lead to the formation of steam, which could cause the pipe to burst.

As the pipe thaws, move the dryer toward the still-frozen areas until the job is complete.

fessional. One thing every homeowner can do, however, regardless of the type of roofing material used on your house, is ensure that your roof can always dry properly.

Remove overhanging tree branches that produce excessive shade and retard drying of the roof surface. Never allow tree branches to strike or rub against the surface of the roof. The branches can break roof shingles or tiles, wear grooves into the surface of the shingles, or loosen the fasteners that hold them. As much as possible, avoid walking on the roof, even when cleaning, inspecting, or repairing it.

Roofing Materials

Residential roofing materials of yesteryear included wood shingles and shakes, composition (asphalt) roofing, metal roofing, and tile. Today's products are constantly evolving to overcome the shortcomings of their predecessors, meet the requirements of the latest building techniques, and comply with increasingly rigorous building codes. Figure 21 illustrates some of the more common roofing materials in use today.

Natural and man-made roofing materials are now rated for fire resistance. Not all products carry a manufacturer's warranty, but those that do typically are covered for a period of 20 to 40 years. Listing the roofing materials used on your home, checking the warranty information, and checking material prices at building supply stores will help you in planning for both minor repairs and the potential, major expense of roof replacement.

Asphalt shingles, the most common and economical roofing material, come in different shapes and a variety of colors and weights. The most popular asphalt styles are strip shingles, interlocking shingles, and large individual shingles.

The asphalt now used to make shingles is actually asphalt flux—a petroleum distillate that binds with the shingle's fibrous core. Older asphalt shingles used cores of organic felts that combined rag, wood, and other cellulose fibers. Newer roofing materials use fiberglass mat reinforcements with plastic binders that firmly bond the inorganic glass fibers. A coarse mineral surfacing gener-

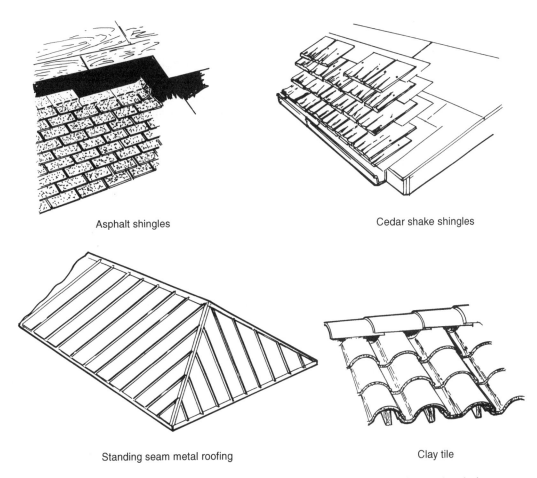

Asphalt shingles

Cedar shake shingles

Standing seam metal roofing

Clay tile

FIGURE 21 Commonly used residential roofing materials: asphalt shingles, cedar shakes, standing seam metal roofing, and clay or concrete tiles. Slate is another commonly used material.

ally covers the exposed areas of asphalt shingles. The granules allow for a wide color selection, help protect the underlying asphalt coating from the damaging effects of prolonged sun exposure, and increase the fire resistance of the shingles.

Laminated two-ply asphalt shingles recently have become popular. Two layers of shingles laminated together provide better protection than one-ply shingles. Most one-ply shingles have a 15- to 20-year limited warranty compared to 25 to 40 years for laminated two-ply shingles. In any event, a typical asphalt roof will last an average of 20 years before you need to consider having it replaced.

Wood shakes and shingles are applied to roofs where the pitch, or slope, is steep enough to ensure proper drainage.

Traditional wood shingles and shakes were cut from logs of red cedar, redwood, cypress, or pine. Western red cedar is by far the most common in existing roofs throughout the U.S. The trees harvested for these logs were old-growth trees, 100 to 800 years old.

Old-style shakes or shingles were individually split or sawed by hand and secured directly to wooden nailing strips with no felt or tarpaper under-layment. Roofs with this type of installation last 25 to 30 years with proper maintenance.

The newer wood shakes and shingles used in residential roofing are made from mixed grain wood, and lack the straight-grained stability and natural rot resistance of the vertical-grained heartwood shakes made from old-growth trees. Building codes now require shakes to be installed on top of tarpaper to prevent leaks. The process does stop leaks, especially if shakes are installed on roofs lacking a steep slope. Unfortunately, the tarpaper also reduces the rate at which the shakes dry out, making them more susceptible to wood rot. Determining the life span of a modern shake roof is an impossible task. Such roofs can last from as little as 6 years to 25 years or more.

Roofing slate is a dense, solid rock selected for its durability and toughness. Impervious to fire, slate also has such a low porosity that it absorbs practically no moisture at all. The finish surface of roofing slate depends on how the slate was split. Most styles have a very smooth, even surface that will readily shed water.

A slate roof is custom designed, engineered, and applied, using custom-made material. Although a slate roof will substantially increase the cost of building a home, there will be no replacement costs because slate lasts. A slate roof is likely to add substantially to the resale value of your home, and with only minor repairs or replacements a slate roof will normally outlast the structure it caps.

Clay tiles have been used as roofing materials since the Bronze Age. Today most clay tiles are made from powdered shale. Clay roofing tiles typically last for 50 years or more. These tiles do not rust or fade and they are noncombustible. Like slate roofs, tile roofs require minimal routine maintenance.

Concrete roofing tiles are made from cement, sand, and water. Concrete tiles offer a less expensive alternative to some other roofing products. Flat concrete tiles in various sizes resemble slate or wooden shakes. Roll tile, also known as barrel or mission tile, resembles clay. As with clay tiles, concrete tiles last a very long time. A properly installed concrete tile roof will, with minor repairs and replacements, last the lifetime of the structure.

Although lightweight, metal roofs are extremely long lasting and over the life of the product the cost is quite reasonable. Metal roofs are adaptable to unique design situations where other roofing products would present problems. The most common metals used for roofing applications are copper, aluminum, zinc, steel, and stainless steel. Finishes applied to these metals range from earth tones to Caribbean pastels.

Routine Care

At least twice a year thoroughly inspect your roof. Spring and autumn are ideal times for routine inspections. Stand on the ground far enough back from the house to allow yourself a good view of one side of your roof. Using a pair of binoculars, look for missing, broken, or torn shingles; exposed underlayment; damaged brick in the chimney; bent gutters; loose or disconnected gutter hangers; and ragged edge lines. Repeat the process to view each side of the roof.

Another spot-check for asphalt roofs is to look closely at the ground where downspouts empty out for the small ceramic granules that coat asphalt shingles. You can expect to find a small quantity of these granules after a rain, but finding large amounts may be a sign that the shingles are aging or have been damaged.

For a closer inspection of the roof, some people get up and walk on the roof or view the roof from a ladder. Do not attempt to walk on a roof unless you are very comfortable with heights and experienced with ladders. Also, walking on shingles can easily damage them. Contract with a qualified roofer to inspect your roof every three years. The roofer can also inspect your skylights for cracks and wear around the seals, caulking, and flashings, making minor repairs as needed to prevent major problems later on.

Signs of a deteriorating shingle roof include cupping (the sides of the shingles roll up toward the center forming a cup-like shape), buckling (the center of the shingle pushes up), loose or missing shingles, and loss of granules. Observing the condition of your roof on a regular basis will alert you to conditions that have changed.

Valley flashing (placed where two sections of roof meet) and step flashing (around chimneys, vent pipes, and other protrusions) also need to be carefully checked. Look for tears, buckling, and chimney shingles that have shifted under the flashing. Because chimneys settle independently from the house, flashing can be vulnerable to damage even in fairly new homes.

When you check the roof from the outside also look over the soffit (the area of the roof that overhangs the house) and ridge vents (at the very peak of the roof) for signs of wear. Remove insect hives or bird nests from vents; these can obstruct the flow of air through the attic.

In cold weather, watch for the formation of ice on the roof. Whether deposited by storms or formed as a result of snow melt, ice is a problem.

Wood shingle roofs are prone to mold growth and are vulnerable to decay, splitting, and curling. Any of these conditions should be dealt with promptly to prevent damage to the sheathing and support members. Take special care to remove all leaf litter, pine needles, or accumulated debris that from between the shingles and shakes and in the valleys of the actual roof structure. If left on the roof, such debris will retain moisture, allowing harmful fungi to grow on the wood, leading to cause wood to rot. Schedule debris removal before the beginning of the wet season. Residents of the Pacific Northwest, for example, may want to schedule this maintenance before the autumn rains begin. If you live in a warm humid climate such as that along the Gulf Coast where molds, mildew, and fungi thrive this task may be required several times each year.

If you choose to hire a professional to clean your roof, do some homework before signing a contract. Be sure the service company will use techniques suitable for your type of roof. For example, using high-pressure washers to remove debris can detach shingles.

Low-slope wood shake and shingle roofs and roofs in hot, humid climates may benefit from application of a surface chemical preservative. Cedar should be allowed to season for approximately one year before it is treated with a chemical preservative. Chemicals may also be applied to destroy and inhibit the re-growth of moss, fungi, and mildew. For best results, apply the chemicals to wet or dampened moss when no rain is forecast for several days following treatment. Thoroughly rinse metal tools, gutters, and flashings that have come in contact with chemical preservatives or fungicides, which can damage metal.

Given the wood's irregular surface, a multi-gallon pump-type sprayer set to produce a coarse spray will result in a more uniform coating. It is better to apply several light coats to obtain good absorption than to try to force the chemicals in all at once. Brushes are also effective because they allow for the thorough treatment of recessed areas and ends.

A properly applied slate roof needs no preservative coatings or cleaning, and weathers better than other roofing materials do. However, you should regularly check the flashings and look for nail pops. Nail pops occur when the nails securing the slates work themselves out of the roof deck underneath the slates and the heads of the nails rise above the surface of the slate. Occasionally, a slate will break. A qualified slate roofer should be called to fix broken slates, nail pops, and flashing in need of repair.

In routine inspections of a clay tile roof be sure to check the flashings, perimeters, and fasteners. Also check the roof and ground after severe storms for loosened, lost, or broken tiles. Should repairs be needed, call in a qualified professional.

Every year, remove accumulated dirt from the surface of a metal roof and inspect it to ensure that flashings and seals are intact. Use a garden hose with a strong water stream to wash the surface of the roof. Begin at the top and work down towards the edges of the roof. (The job goes easier, and starting at the top is safer.) Inspect crimped areas with care, looking for early signs of rust. If you decide to paint your roof, be sure to select an appropriate paint formulated specifically for use on metal roofs.

Metal dents when hit with enough force. Falling branches, hailstorms, or other unavoidable events will damage part of the roof. If this occurs, take a look at the damage. Small dents in the crimped ridges may be fairly easy to straighten out with pliers. Go slowly and be careful not to crack or tear the metal. Tiny cracks may be caulked, filled, or patched. If necessary, a metal roofer will be able to remove the damaged portion of the roof and replace it. With normal care, a sheet metal roof should last from 20 to 50 years.

Flat Roofs

Inspect flat roofs frequently. Cracks or tears in the roofing membrane, blisters, or wrinkles can all jeopardize the integrity of the roof, making flat roofs prone to moisture problems. After rainstorms, sweep areas that retain puddles of water to help them dry faster and reduce the likelihood of water infiltration.

Also, after heavy snows or ice storms, flat roofs should be manually cleared. Gravity takes care of this maintenance chore by pulling heavy loads off roofs with a steeper slope. Although low-slope and flat roofs are designed to hold substantial weight, wet snow and ice can be deceptively heavy and can place tremendous strain on the roof.

When clearing a flat roof of snow and ice, remember that the roofing material itself is relatively delicate. Scraping the surface of the roof with a snow shovel or chipper can easily damage the shingles or roofing membrane and can result in leaks. A roof rake is designed to push the snow off low slope and flat roofs. A roof rake has a long pole and the head of the rake is fitted with a rubber blade. The long pole allows you to safely reach most areas of a snow-covered roof from the ground. Using a roof rake is fairly simple but you should keep in mind some basic rules:

1. Before beginning, survey the ground beneath the roof to be sure you won't crush expensive landscaping with falling snowloads.
2. Don't use a roof rake—or any implement—where electrical lines may be contacted. Simply stay away from sections of the roof where power lines connect to the house. Touching these lines with any tool, pole, or body part may result in serious injury or even death. In most situations removing snow from areas you can safely reach will adequately lighten the load on your roof.
3. Always start at the ridge line of the roof and pull straight down toward the eave edge. Never push snow up from the eave edge toward the ridge; pushing upward forces snow under the shingles and can damage the underlayment and decking.

Pull the snow completely off the roof. Do not allow snow to pile up on the gutters. Besides increasing the risk of ice dams, the heavy snow may warp the gutter or pull it away from the roof.

Deciding Whether to Repair or Replace the Roof

Barring any natural disasters, most of the roofing material used in home construction will provide many years of service before requiring major work. Some

Snow on Roof: Snow is very heavy, weighing anywhere from 10 to 50 pounds per cubic foot. Building codes in some areas of the country require that roofs be designed to hold as much as 400 pounds per square foot. A well-designed house can withstand the weight of snow. However, it is a good idea to clear snow off flat roofs, especially if the roof design is not suited to withstand a heavy snowfall.

of the more obvious signs that a new roof is needed are weather-worn and damaged shingles with curled-up edges.

Curling shingles (Figure 22) signal that roofing material is drying up and becoming brittle. Curled edges no longer properly cover the roof area beneath them, and the dry shingles crack easily, allowing moisture to penetrate to the roof deck. Replace curled shingles as soon as possible to prevent leaks. If more than just a few shingles are dog-eared, consider a new roof.

A leak that occurs only when rain is being driven at an angle warrants a call to a professional roofer. Chances are the seals between the shingles have failed, and major renovations are needed. If most of the granules have worn off your shingles, you need a new roof. Your fire protection is gone. If unexplained water damage occurs on inside walls and ceilings as shown in Figure 23, it's time to call in a professional.

The choice of whether to repair, replace, or re-roof is more than just a question of economics. Re-roofing, in which new shingles are applied directly over existing ones, typically costs about 60 percent of the price of having the old roof torn off and replaced. With re-roofing, the home gets a roof that looks new again, does not leak, and will provide decades of additional service. Unfortunately, not all roofs are suitable candidates for re-roofing; and if the decision is made in haste, the roof may fail again within a short period of time.

When considering a major home expense like this, don't rush. Consult several professional roofers before making a decision. Most roofing contractors will inspect the inside and outside of the roof, give you an opinion, and provide an estimate at no charge. Ask each to explain their recommendation.

One concern is the overall condition of the existing roof: If it needs extensive prep work, replacement may prove less expensive than re-roofing. Check for signs of extensive blistering or tearing, corroded mechanical fasteners, or signs of ponding (standing puddles of water), evidenced by concentric rings of dirt or mineral deposits on the roof surface. Check the surface of the roof for

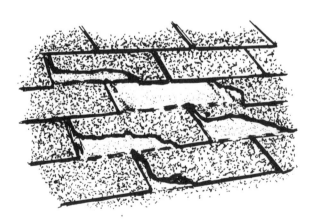

Damaged and worn shingles

FIGURE 22 An example of damaged asphalt shingles.

FIGURE 23 The source of the water damage to this wall was not the window but a roof leak. Source: Original photograph by James Gerhart.

signs of structural movement such as split membranes, stressed expansion joints, or buckled flashings. Unless corrected, this movement will lead to premature failure of the new roof. Inspect the attic for signs of rusting fasteners or structural components as well as rot and other deterioration. If a section of wood decking appears questionable, test it by gently pushing an ice pick or similar object into the wood. If the pick goes in easily you may have serious moisture problems.

Safety

No matter how careful you try to be, accidents will happen. However, you can take steps—both in your everyday life and in the way you approach home maintenance projects—to reduce the likelihood and lessen the impact of accidents. Steps you can take include the following:

- Equip your house with smoke and carbon monoxide detectors and fire extinguishers.
- Regularly check detectors and extinguishers to be sure they function properly; replace batteries on battery-operated units at least twice a year.
- Keep a well-stocked first-aid kit handy.
- Keep locks on doors and windows in good operating condition.
- Memorize and practice emergency evacuation procedures.

- Post a written list of emergency contacts near telephones.
- Identify the safety shutoff switches for major appliances and know how to use them (or simply know not to bypass them).
- Identify the main and site-specific shutoff valves for natural gas and water supplies.
- Use hibachis, charcoal grills, and appliances with internal combustion engines only outdoors.
- Call utilities to identify locations of buried lines before digging on your property.
- Repair malfunctioning systems promptly, particularly if they involve major systems of the house (such as the HVAC system or electrical system).
- Work in well-ventilated areas.
- Once or twice a year, check storage spaces to identify and properly dispose of flammable items (including cleaning products) that are no longer useful.
- Store products that pose potential fire hazards with care; for example, do not store oily rags from painting or varnishing in the house or in attached structures.
- Buy or rent proper equipment and materials.
- Plan ahead. Figure out where you and your tools will need to be at various points in the task, and how you will position them to make the job go quickly, efficiently, and safely.
- Keep tools and equipment clean, dry, and free of rust, and sharpen blades as necessary (dull blades can be more dangerous than sharp ones).
- Store equipment and materials properly and in an organized fashion. Doing this reduces waste, protects the environment, and reduces the hazards posed by chemical fumes or potential fires or explosions.
- Use extension cords of adequate lengths and ratings for the task at hand.
- Check and replace damaged or frayed electrical cords.
- Use three-pronged extension cords to accept three-pronged tools; modifying two-pronged extension cords can easily result in electrical fire or shock.
- Use safety glasses or goggles.
- Use dust or particle masks or respirators to protect you from breathing paint chips, dust particles, and chemical stripper fumes.
- Use sturdy work gloves, which provide an extra layer of protection between your skin and sharp tools or chemical strippers. This can mean the difference between a trip to the emergency room and merely replacing a pair of gloves.
- Use firm-soled shoes or boots to protect your feet, reduce foot fatigue, and maintain the natural arch in the foot when standing on ladders or other precarious spots.
- Store putty knives, hammers, screwdrivers, and all other tools properly while working. An ill-placed tool can easily cause a fall.
- Use a toolbelt. (Toolbelts are convenient and can save you trips up and down ladders.)

- Use a lockable toolbox. Children or visitors may be injured by tools left lying about. Store these items in the toolbox when you are not using them.
- Clean up your work area and lock up your tools and equipment when you finish work each day.
- Use power tools only in areas where there is no standing water and when there is no threat of an electrical storm.
- Unplug power tools before changing accessories and when you are not using them. (Current may flow through the cord even if the tool is not switched on.)
- Use ear protection when running power tools. (Close proximity to running power tools without ear protection can cause long-term hearing damage.)
- Read and follow manufacturer's instructions for the operation, cleaning, and care of appliances and equipment—especially power equipment.
- Take breaks; don't keep working when you are exhausted.
- When working from heights, always work with a partner on the ground. Besides securing the ladder and handing up tools or materials, your partner is there to help you should an emergency occur.
- Respect gravity. Avoid the temptation to over-extend your reach when working from a ladder. Doing so will shift your body weight and make the ladder unstable.
- Make safety a top priority when working on a roof—even one with a relatively flat pitch. Every year people sustain serious, disabling, and even fatal injuries by failing to use common-sense precautions while working from ladders or on roofs.
- Work from the ground as much as possible, using extension tools as necessary to minimize the time you must spend on ladders, scaffolding, or on the roof.
- Keep your feet on the floor, your body weight balanced, and don't overextend your reach when working from inside a window.
- Place materials in locations where they will not cause a fall, injure people, or damage property.
- Take the time to properly anchor safety equipment such as lifelines, lanyards, or safety harnesses. (Taking this step may seem like a hassle, but it can make the difference between a bad scare and a lifetime of pain or worse in the event of a fall.)
- Ask your builder if safety anchors have been left on the roof from installation. If anchors are in place, test them each time you inspect the roof.
- When working on a roof, keep safety lines adjusted so the maximum distance you could fall at any time is no more than 6 feet.

Besides protecting yourself, following common-sense precautions and using proper safety equipment—or requiring contract workers to do so—also helps protect your interests should you need to file for insurance or protect yourself legally in the event of an accident.

Septic Tanks—See Plumbing

Siding

Most residential siding consists of wood, aluminum, steel, vinyl, or other synthetic materials, often with decorative accents in brick or stone. The trade-offs in the various materials and finishes tend to be in durability and ease of maintenance. Wood siding is extremely durable, for example, but may require repainting every four to six years. Vinyl siding needs no painting, but may begin to fade over time. Many synthetic siding materials carry guarantees against cracking, chipping, peeling and termites for periods of ten years or more. Siding made from coated plywood or plastic finished wood may be guaranteed for the life of the house.

Routine Care

Aluminum and vinyl siding need regular cleanings. Dirt and grime can adhere to and stain vinyl siding and trim, particularly if the surface is textured. Scrub vinyl products using a moderately stiff bristle broom and a solution of water and a mild soap. Do not use a wire brush; the wire brush will scratch the surface of the siding.

In most vinyl installations, each course of siding is locked into the one above it. Move the bristles across the siding horizontally. Scrubbing with a vertical movement may dislodge the locking mechanism. Light horizontal scrubbing should be enough to loosen the dirt so that the pressure from a garden hose will rinse it away. Loosened vinyl or aluminum siding is best repaired or replaced by a qualified installer. Check behind the loose siding before securing it to make sure there are no signs of water damage. If you use a power washer, have a care not to apply too much pressure, forcing water between the courses.

Wood siding must be painted, stained, or sealed to protect it against the elements (see Painting). However, too-frequent paintings or a too-thick application can lead to premature surface cracking and peeling. Worn, cracked, or peeling areas need scraping and repainting to prevent moisture penetration and rot.

Ice that forms between layers of siding can force clapboards away from the wall, resulting in *nail pops*. To reset a popped nail, use a hammer and *nail punch* to drive the nail back into position flush with the siding material. (The nail punch gives you precise control and keeps the hammer head from striking and marring the surface of the siding material.)

Repeated freezing and thawing may work a clapboard back and forth, widening the nailhole. In this situation drive a new nail close to the original hole, fill the original hole with a dab of latex caulk, and touch up the repair with paint that matches the original color of the siding.

Smoke Detectors

Smoke detectors have become a standard, necessary piece of equipment for every home. Today approximately 93 percent of homes have one or more of these devices. Being familiar with and maintaining the smoke detectors in your home greatly increases your chance of surviving a house fire.

Types of Smoke Detectors

Ionization smoke detectors contain small amounts of radioactive material that *ionizes* air as it passes through the smoke chamber, creating a very small electrical charge. Although they can be tiny, the particles present in smoke interfere with the ionization so air containing smoke particles will carry a smaller charge. When the level of ionization declines to a preset ratio it triggers the detector's alarm. The radioactive material in this type of smoke detector is harmless and generates little more than normal background radiation. Ionization detectors are even sensitive to the tiny, nearly invisible smoke particles produced by hot, blazing fires.

A *photoelectric* smoke detector emits a continuous beam of light. Smoke particles reflect the light back into the photoelectric cell, triggering the alarm. Photoelectric smoke detectors respond more readily to the larger particles in smoke that are commonly produced by a cooler, smoldering fire.

Hard-wired and battery-powered models are available for both ionization and photoelectric detectors. Which is best for your home depends on several factors:

- desired placement of the detectors
- your ability to follow a schedule of testing
- the likelihood of power failures, which affect hard-wired detectors

Battery-powered smoke detectors are easy to install. Once the unit is in position, slip in a battery, test it, and secure the lid. Change batteries twice a year to ensure proper operation. Many people schedule battery changes for the days we change from daylight savings and back to standard time. A battery-operated smoke detector that begins to *beep* needs fresh batteries.

Smoke detector that are hard wired to a home's household electric current have a continuous power source as long as the circuit to which they are connected has current flowing through it. Some hard-wired detectors incorporate a backup battery to keep the unit running in the event of a power outage. Replace backup batteries twice a year.

If you are experienced with performing electrical work, installing a hard-wired smoke detector is relatively simple. Remember to turn off the power at the circuit breaker before you begin work. Homeowners inexperienced with electrical work should call an electrician.

Routine Care

Vacuum smoke detectors at least once a month. Dust, cobwebs, even insects can get into the units and hinder their performance. Also push the test button in and hold until the alarm sounds.

Some people prefer to replace smoke detectors every few years, just to be on the safe side. When you purchase a smoke detector, note the manufacturer's information. A typical life expectancy for a standalone unit is about 10 to 12 years.

▶ **Storm Doors and Windows—See Doors, Windows**

Termites and Other Insect Pests

American homeowners spend approximately $1 billion a year to replace wood damaged by termites. A much wiser investment is an annual professional inspection that results in prompt preventive treatment as needed. A professional exterminator will check:

- any places where wood meets the ground
- cracks in the foundation
- areas where the ground is not at least 3 inches below the top of the foundation
- any area with a negative slope
- areas under damaged or clogged gutters
- landscaping that retains moisture close to the foundation
- slab foundations wherever a pipe penetrates the slab

Termites need water to survive. The more moisture available around the home's foundation, the more likely a termite problem could develop.

Checking for Signs of Termite Problems

Be aware of three signs that indicate the presence of termites:

1. Piles of translucent wings around windows and doors: Termites avoid direct sunlight but are attracted to the light that shines through doors or windows at night. During flight they frequently shed their wings.
2. Mud tubes: Termites must remain moist to survive. To cross open areas termites construct protective tubes that shelter them from drying air and daylight (see Figure 24).
3. Wood damage: Termites eat wood from the inside out, which makes detection difficult. Check exposed wood members by trying to push an ice pick into them. If the pick goes into the wood with little effort, you've got problems.

Treating a Termite Problem

Treatment for active termite infestations involves putting physical and chemical barriers between the termites and the house. Usually a small trench about 6 to 8 inches deep is dug around the outside perimeter of the foundation. The trench is filled with a liquid chemical that saturates the soil, then filled back in. With some foundations holes must be drilled through the concrete

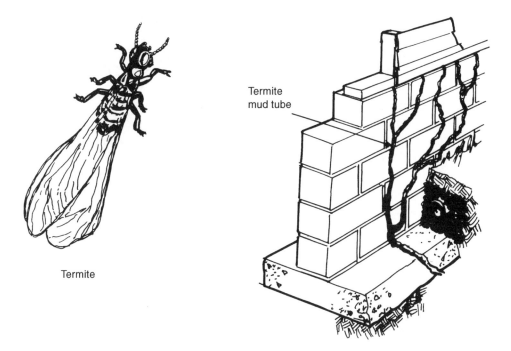

FIGURE 24 Close-up view of a termite and the sheltering tubes they travel through when crossing exposed areas.

to reach the earth below. The chemical treatment is then forced through the holes into the soil beneath the foundation. Foundation cracks also are treated with pressurized infusion. Physical barriers vary, but the principle is always to prevent any direct wood-to-ground contact. How long will a professional termite proofing treatment last? Treatment may last up to five years—but homes in damp climates may need more frequent re-treatments.

Homeowners may inadvertently attract termites by:

- building or repairing porches, decks, or steps with untreated wood
- stacking firewood against the foundation
- allowing dirt to mound up around the foundation
- allowing vapor barriers in crawl spaces to become damaged
- leaving wood scraps under the house in crawl spaces

Beyond Termites

Professional exterminators also can check and treat for carpenter ants, carpenter bees, powder post beetles, wasps, and hornets. Each of these insects can cause some damage to a house, although none is as devastating as the termite.

In most areas of the country termite inspection and treatment may be required for home insurance or before the home may be sold. The pest-control company may have separate treatment contracts covering different kinds of insect pests, for example termites and powder-post beetles. If you own a home susceptible to problems with more than one type of damaging insect, be sure to keep all relevant treatment contracts up to date, and don't rely on treatment for one type of insect to control them all.

Because most pest-control treatments involve powerful, long-lasting chemicals and poisons, they can pose a potential health hazard should vapors be inhaled, or dirt or materials containing the chemicals be handled or ingested. Professional exterminators know how to apply these chemicals properly and safely; however, homeowners are wise to respect the potential hazards involved. Families with small children and pets should take precautions to keep children and animals away from immediate treatment areas both during and after treatment.

Professional exterminators can provide specific information about the materials they use, including known risk factors, safety precautions, and less-toxic alternatives. Homeowners who purchase over-the-counter pest-control products should read labels carefully and abide by the manufacturer's instructions for each product's safe use, storage, and disposal (see also Household Chemicals).

▶ **Tile (Wall)—See Walls**

▶ **Toilets—See Plumbing**

Trees and Shrubs

Trees and shrubs help personalize your yard. One of the most frequent errors new homeowners make when planting shrubs, trees, and hedges is failing to consider the mature size of the plant. The small shrub you plant today can grow considerably and, if planted too close to the house, may cause problems down the road. Roots may invade pipes; planting and mulch may disrupt grading; leaves may clog gutters; and shaded, mulched soil retains moisture close to the foundation.

Rather than have to move (and traumatize) a tree or shrub as it matures, plant it where it will have room to grow. To keep moisture, mold, and mildew problems to a minimum, place trees and shrubs at least 5 feet from the house.

Routine Care

Proper care of trees and woody shrubs requires an understanding of some fundamentals. The root systems that support and feed trees are expansive, complex networks that extend one and a half to five times the diameter of the tree's canopy, mostly within 3 feet of the surface. Thinning topsoil or indiscriminate digging can damage the root systems of trees and shrubs. When planting, dig wide, not deep. A wide hole backfilled with loosened soil allows roots to spread out and anchor the growing tree. Native soil is best for backfill unless the soil is poisoned, of poor quality, or high in clay (which can harden and entrap roots).

Bark also is essential to the plant's health. When bark is cut, chipped, or otherwise damaged, underlying tissues become susceptible to potentially fatal disease and insect infestation. Trees have special cells that secrete materials to seal off wounds to the bark. Proper pruning and trimming techniques take advantage of this self-sealing quality to minimize damage to the tree.

For our purposes *pruning* and *trimming* will be treated as the same process. Most homeowners prune trees and shrubs to improve their health or to suit an aesthetic goal.

Pruning for health involves removing diseased or insect-infested wood, thinning the crown to increase airflow and reduce pest problems, and removing crossing and rubbing branches. Pruning encourages trees to develop a strong, aesthetically pleasing structure, lowers the risk of storm damage, and can even stimulate flower production. Pruning to remove broken or damaged limbs also encourages wound closure.

When pruning by hand, use sharp tools that can cut branches cleanly without tearing. (It's better for the tree and safer for you.) Make cuts at a *node* (the point at which one branch or twig attaches to another). Spring growth begins at buds, and twigs grow until a new node is formed. To encourage wound healing remove only branch tissue; do not damage *stem* (trunk) tissue.

Look for the *branch collar* that grows from the stem tissue at the underside of the base of the branch. The upper surface of the collar is a bark ridge that usually runs more or less parallel to the branch angle. Begin your pruning cut just outside the branch bark ridge and angle it down, away from the stem of the tree, to avoid injuring the branch collar.

Retain branches with strong U-shaped angles of attachment. Remove branches with narrow, V-shaped angles of attachment. The latter tend to form something called *included bark* (a wedge of inward-rolled bark between two branches). Take care not to prune too much: Remove no more than one-fourth of a tree's living branches at one time. *Crown raising,* the removal of branches from the bottom of the crown of a tree to provide clearance for pedestrians, vehicles, buildings, or sight lines, may be specified for street trees by municipal ordinance. In some localities the municipal governments themselves arrange for crown raising as needed to comply with these ordinances. Never prune trees that are touching or near utility lines; instead, consult your local utility company.

Chemical Scents: Recently wounded trees emit chemical scents that attract insects, which may carry diseases such as Dutch elm or oak wilt. Pruning elms, oaks, and other trees during the correct time of year helps prevent the spread of these and other fatal diseases.

Schedule pruning work for times that don't impede the growth and healing periods of trees and shrubs. For most species, pruning during the dormant season (usually late fall or winter) works best, but there are some exceptions. Use this table as a general guide and check with a local nursery if you need advice about pruning a specific species.

Type of Tree	Examples	When to Prune
Conifers	Firs, pines	Any time of year, but pruning during dormant season minimizes sap and resin flow.
Early bloomers	Redbud, dogwood	In spring immediately after flowering, as buds will form on new twigs during next growing season.
Summer or autumn bloomers		In dormant season—flower buds will form on new twigs during next growing season.
Trees susceptible to fireblight	Crabapple, hawthorn, pear, mountain ash, flowering quince, Pyracantha	In dormant season, to reduce likelihood of bacterial infection.
Nonflowering trees	Oaks, maples, ash	In dormant season—you can see tree structure and wounds will close during next growing season, reducing chance of disease.

Remove dead branches at any time of year. If trees are seriously wounded from storms or from necessary but untimely pruning, wound dressings can help protect the tree against infection. Wound dressings will not stop decay or cure diseases—and may actually interfere with the tree's self-protective healing process—so they should not be used with routine pruning.

Apply tree and shrub food (lawn food won't do) about three to four weeks before spring bud breaks to allow the food to enter the soil and be absorbed. Water-soluble fertilizers work best for followup applications given later in the spring or summer. Fertilizers slightly high in nitrogen will encourage rapid leaf development.

Mulching is not essential in many yards, but may be helpful to conserve moisture, control weeds, or prevent soil erosion. Keep mulch away from the tree base lest the retained moisture encourage potential overgrowth of molds and bacteria.

Most areas of the U.S. experience enough rainfall during a typical summer to satisfy the basic water needs of yard plantings. However, using a sprinkler during lengthy dry spells or in drier areas helps ensure plantings remain

A Note to New Homeowners: When new plantings are introduced alongside existing trees or shrubs, the newer plants draw nutrients and water from soil that previously nourished the trees and shrubs. Given the trend to preserve existing trees on newer building sites, your yard is likely to include a mix of old and new vegetation right from the start. Adding your own landscaping for aesthetic reasons further complicates the mix.

If you notice signs of stress (unusual loss or discoloration of bark or leaves, dying branches, and so forth) act swiftly. Discover and treat contributing causes as well as outward symptoms. Solutions may include moving or thinning out surrounding plants, providing more (or less) water, or enriching the soil to better sustain the existing mix of trees and plants.

If you are not an expert landscaper, obtain sound advice from a nursery before you add plantings, especially if you will plant near existing trees or shrubs. Discuss the short- and long-term needs of the new plants and where you will place them in relation to existing trees and structures.

hydrated. During prime growing months, trees and shrubs often require the equivalent of an inch of rainfall per week.

▷ **Vinyl Siding—See Siding**

▷ **Wallpaper—See Walls**

Walls

Your home has two types of walls: load bearing and partition. Load-bearing walls support part of the weight of the house. Partition walls define interior living spaces, although some may also be load bearing. Go down to your basement or up to your attic and look to see which way the floor joists run; bearing walls always run perpendicular to joists, while non-bearing walls usually run parallel.

Walls have been traditionally framed with structural wood such as 2 × 4 inch timbers, although metal (steel) framing is increasingly accepted as a substitute for wood. In framing a *bottom plate* (horizontal wood or metal member) is secured to the floor, vertical studs are attached to this plate (usually at 16-inch or 24-inch intervals), and the whole is capped with a *top plate.* Bearing walls usually have a double top plate. The space between the studs is called a *stud cavity.*

Exterior walls are always load-bearing walls. The outside part of these walls is usually sheathed in sheets of insulating material that provide protection from temperature variation inside the home. This insulation also provides a stiff backing for the exterior finish materials such as siding, stone, brick, or stucco. Additional insulation, electrical and home automation wiring, telephone and television cables, and plumbing lines are placed within the stud cavities.

The interior side of an exterior wall—and both sides of most partition walls—will be finished with sheets of gypsum wallboard and a coat of material that resembles plaster, which can be painted or wallpapered. Alternative interior wall finishes include exposed brick (or brick veneer), stucco, or paneling.

Because partition walls face interior spaces on both sides, lighter weight insulation is used. Insulation in interior walls provides the home with better zone temperature control and helps reduce noise by deadening sound transference from one living space to another.

Wall Coverings

Wall coverings come in many colors, patterns, and textures, making them a popular choice for decorating.

Bathrooms and kitchens need moisture-resistant wall coverings that can stand up to regular scrubbing. Vinyl wallpaper or heavy-duty washable wallpaper are practical choices.

Natural wood, or a product made to look like wood, can warm up the look of a room like no other material. Printed hardboards are available in many colors and designs, including wood grains. Hardboard is easier to care for than real wood, which requires a seal of urethane or another water-resistant coating. Veneers backed by plywood are popular choices, as are planks such as barnboards and tongue-and-groove boards. Most interior paneling is stain resistant and easy to clean. Wood paneling may need a wood cleaner, but most synthetics (and wood coated with a synthetic finish) usually can be cleaned using a cloth and a mild detergent solution.

Moisture in Walls

Water stains or cracked and peeling interior wall finishes signal a moisture problem. Settling may cause cracks, but peeling or staining are your clues that the problem involves water.

Walls can become repositories for water from roof leaks or water penetrating from doorways or window openings. Besides addressing the visible repair tasks to fix damaged finishes, prompt attention to the root causes of water problems is needed to prevent more trouble—and potentially expensive repair—down the road.

Tile

Tile makes an excellent choice for kitchen and bathroom walls, which need special protection from moisture. Tub and shower surrounds must be waterproof, not just water-resistant. Applied to wallboard, plaster, or plywood surfaces, ceramic tiles can last a lifetime.

Wall tiles are normally glossier than floor tiles, adding to their beauty and making them easier to clean. Glazed tile (or bricks, for that matter) typically wash clean with simple soap and water. Stubborn discolorations usually can be removed with a nonabrasive household cleanser. Special tile cleaners also are available.

Routine Care

Routine care of interior walls generally involves little more than occasional cleaning and repainting the surface using products and materials appropriate to the specific wall surface (see Cleaning Interior and Exterior Surfaces; also Painting).

Minor repairs to interior walls typically include such tasks as resetting popped nails, filling nail holes, and patching small cracks or abrasions in wallboard. Deeper cracks or gouges may be filled by first spackling, covering the patch with a fiberglass mesh, then applying a thin covering layer of spackle that can be lightly sanded to feather it into the wall for a smooth finish. (The mesh helps keep the spackling compound from sagging or cracking open after drying.)

If finished wallboard on a partition wall sustains major damage, you can cut out the damaged section and fit in a replacement piece using special tape and a plaster-like compound available at your local home supply store. Wallboard can be purchased in single sheets and is not difficult to cut to size.

If interior walls show signs of major or continuing problems with moisture, seek professional help. Elevated moisture levels within walls can lead to potential hazards by attracting insects, promoting the growth of molds and mildew, reducing the effectiveness of insulation, and damaging multiple layers of materials within the wall. Electrical shorts are another potential concern, particularly in houses with aging wiring that may have become frayed or damaged.

Water Heaters

Gas, electric, and oil-fueled water heaters all have a control mechanism to govern water temperature. The safest setting is at 120° F or lower. The lower setting will also result in lower energy bills, as will placing an insulation jacket on the heater tank. (On gas heaters, be sure the jacket does not block air intake.) Reducing the temperature of the water may also help alleviate noise caused by steam in the pipes.

As shown in Figure 25 two water lines—one hot, one cold—branch out from the water heater through the house to serve the various fixtures and water-using appliances. The smaller size of these supply lines helps sustain the pressure necessary to carry water throughout your home.

An electric water heater can be expected to function well with minimal maintenance for about 14 years. Gas appliances last almost as long, on average from 11 to 13 years.

Routine Care

To properly maintain your hot water heater, periodically drain off a few gallons of water to remove rust and mineral deposits from the bottom of the tank. Disconnect the power source before attaching a garden hose to the faucet on the appliance. Slowly open the faucet and allow the water to run until clear. Drain

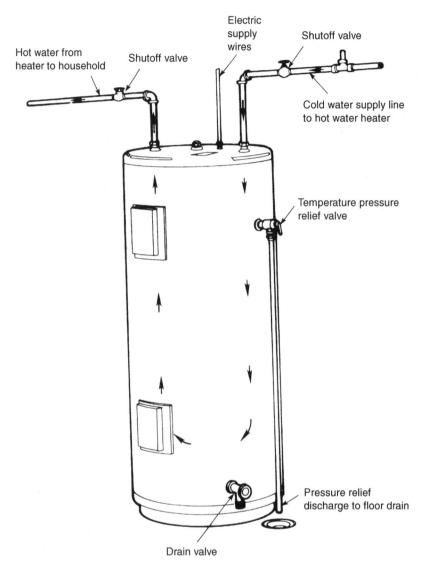

FIGURE 25 A common electric water heater showing the exterior components and water flow into and out of the tank.

off several gallons of water. Even if it comes out clear, it's likely to have high concentrations of dissolved mineral sediment. Draining the tank once or twice a year is especially important for efficient functioning of gas units. If the unit uses a standing flame pilot light, be sure to follow the manufacturer's instructions exactly when relighting the pilot. If you have hard water, installing a water softener also can help keep mineral deposits from clogging water heaters and other equipment.

If you have a gas-powered water heater, do not store flammable materials or chemicals near the unit. Fumes escaping from stored chemicals may become concentrated until the unit's pilot can ignite them, causing a dangerous gas explosion.

Every three months or so, check the temperature and pressure relief valve on your water heater to be sure the lever works properly. If the thermostat should fail, the valve can prevent a dangerous increase in water temperature and pressure.

When to Call in a Professional

When you notice lower hot water temperatures or less hot water, call in a professional plumber to check the inside of the tank. The plumber can clean out stubborn mineral deposits, scale, and rust, check the heating element or burner, and if necessary replace damaged parts.

If you add a bathroom to your home or add appliances that use hot water, you may need to upgrade your water heater to a larger-size tank in order to handle the potentially increased demand. Consult with your remodeler or plumber and don't forget to factor this cost into your budget when you are considering such an addition.

▶ **Water Pipes—See Plumbing**

Weatherstripping

Even in new, tightly built homes little cracks and crevices can lead to loss of air you have paid to heat or cool. Most homes average a half a mile of cracks— in terms of exposure, the equivalent of leaving a window open all year round.

Every house is designed to have some degree of air exchange with the outside. Air exchanges help exhaust humidity and indoor pollutants that build up inside. A home with an exchange rate somewhere between 0.5 and 1.0 air exchanges per hour is considered a well-sealed house. An air leak obvious enough to produce a draft is more than you need—and simple to detect and correct. Leaks of this sort usually occur above or below windows or doors or at connecting points such as where walls abut door or window frames. Leaks around windows and doors can be stopped using weatherstripping or caulk.

A variety of colored caulking compounds are available to work with most colors and styles of trim. Using a caulking gun apply a bead of caulk smoothly and evenly along the seam where the window or door frame meets the wall. To even out the bead, dip your finger into water and with light pressure run your finger along the bead from one end to the other. (If you don't want to use your finger, try the rounded handle of a wooden spatula or spoon. Moisten the wood so it won't drag too hard against the caulk.)

Types of Weatherstripping

To choose the most suitable type of weatherstripping, consider the following factors:

- To what type of surface will the weatherstripping be attached? Foam might be appropriate where the sash of a double-hung window meets the frame, but it would wear out quickly in the tracks of a sliding glass window.

■ How often is the door or window used? A frequently used door calls for a more durable weatherstripping than one that is rarely opened.

■ Plain *door sweeps* have a flexible felt or plastic strip that rests against and sweeps across the threshold. Door sweeps attach to the outside bottom edge of doors with glue, screws, or nails.

■ *Magnetic stops* incorporate a magnetic strip inside a vinyl gasket. When attached to the inside bottom of a metal-clad door, the strip creates an airtight seal when the door is closed.

■ *Pile weatherstripping* is a self-adhesive or snap-in strip often used to replace factory-installed weatherstripping on any type of door or window.

■ *Felt weatherstripping* is normally used to seal narrow gaps around windows and doors. It is generally fastened with tacks or staples to the inside edges of the door or window frame.

■ *Closed-cell foam weatherstripping* is self-adhesive and used primarily on hinged windows, double-hung window sashes, and doors.

■ *Open-cell foam weatherstripping* is typically used on interior doors that are infrequently used. This self-adhesive type of weatherstripping is less durable but effective at reducing drafts within the house.

■ *Metal-backed felt or vinyl weatherstripping* is secured with nails and is used to replace factory-installed weatherstripping on door frames. Because of the metal backing and the nails used in installation these products are best used in dry environments. *Metal-reinforced foam-filled gaskets* are used most often on doors and on the inside and outside of double-hung windows.

■ *Ribbed weatherstripping* is designed for sealing rather narrow gaps in window and door frames.

■ *Spring-tension metal weatherstripping* is durable and used for both windows and doors, but it lacks the flexibility of some other products.

■ *V-strip weatherstripping* is self-adhesive and works well with sliding doors or windows.

■ *Nail-on tubular gaskets* frequently are used to seal irregular gaps around exterior windows and doors and are nailed into position.

■ *Threshold inserts* attack the problem of air leaks from a different angle. The inserts attach directly to the existing threshold, building up the threshold to meet the bottom of the door.

Most types of weatherstripping are easy to install—using pliers, a hammer, and the right nails or a strong water-resistant household glue. Properly installed, the weatherstripping will not interfere with the motion of the door or window.

▶ Window Air Conditioners—See Air-Conditioning Systems

Windows

Numerous styles of windows are used in new construction. Framing materials include aluminum, steel, wood, solid vinyl, and vinyl-clad wood. Most of the newer styles are double-glazed or even triple-glazed for greater energy efficiency. Most double- and triple-glazed window styles do not require separate storm windows.

A double-glazed window has two panes of glass with a sealed air space between them. The air space acts as an insulator, dramatically reducing heating and cooling costs while also reducing noise transfer. Triple-glazed windows (three panes of glass with two sealed air spaces) afford even greater efficiencies. Some window styles use inert gases such as argon and krypton between the glass panes as a more efficient insulator.

Insulated glass generally carries a warranty, often five to ten years, against defects and seal failure. Check seals when you inspect insulated windows: this is the area where most problems will appear. One clue to problems with the seal is fogging between the panes.

Storm Windows

Windows with integrated storm window units are simple to put into place. Usually side latches on the left and right of the storm window sash allow you to release or reposition the storm window.

Traditional removable storm windows still provide protection for single-glazed windows. Traditional storm windows attach to the outside of the window and may be held to the window frame or siding by screws or by a series of clips that fasten into the frame. Figure 26 shows the construction of a typical storm window. A strip of man-made material is installed as a *weather break* where the outside sash meets the inside sash. Felt strips are often placed strategically around the inside of the sash to act as weatherstripping.

Routine Care

The very nature of windows makes them vulnerable to weathering. Exposure is likely to wear down different parts of the window at different rates, and the variety of materials used in windows can mean a wide variation in longevity.

Refresh painted wood or steel surfaces every few years. Use a glossy exterior paint on wood, rust-inhibiting paint on steel. Have a care not to paint windows shut—a frequent mistake of novices. To avoid this problem, paint the window in stages and apply relatively thin coats at each stage. Aluminum, vinyl, and vinyl-clad windows do not need painting. Aluminum frames will turn gray over time, but if you prefer the brighter new look a coat of wax will slow the oxidation that causes the graying. Glazing may easily last for 20 years, screens for 25 to 50 years, aluminum casements for 10 to 20 years, and wood casements for 20 to 50 years or even longer if well maintained and not directly exposed to the elements.

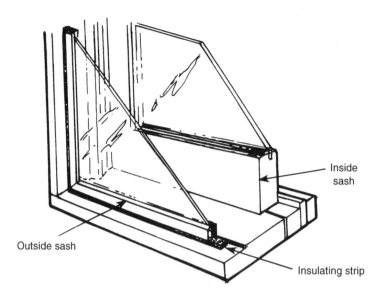

Inside
sash

Outside sash

Insulating strip

FIGURE 26 Weather breaks built into a storm window prevent temperature transference.

Routine care of windows involves cleaning and checking the operation of the window and the various parts of the window, sash, sills, and trim for signs of wear and damage.

In air-conditioned homes nowadays, windows stay shut most of the time—so it's easy to overlook simple maintenance tasks. Spring and fall are good times both to clean windows and to check them for proper fit and operation.

Remove accumulated dirt and grime on outside surfaces of doors and windows on a regular basis. Commercial glass cleaners are fine for the glass, but the ammonia in many glass-cleaning products will remove the shine from gloss paints.

Exterior glass also can be cleaned using crumpled newspaper and a solution of equal parts vinegar and water or 3 tablespoons of denatured alcohol per quart of warm water. For lighter cleaning jobs, try a solution of 1 cup of vinegar to 1 gallon of water, applied and wiped off using a sponge or lintless cloth.

Painted, stained, or varnished wood surfaces are best cleaned using a solution of mild soap and water followed by a thorough rinsing with clean water. On flat horizontal surfaces such as sills or thresholds, use a stiff broom to sweep away excess water that remains after cleaning. Marble window sills require specialized cleaners.

Moisture from water, snow, and ice can warp wooden windows, and ice can damage metal tracks. Harsh weather also can deteriorate the finish of painted surfaces such as frames or sashes. Time, weathering, and wear also can cause the glazing compound in wood windows to become brittle and crumble away (particularly in single-paned styles).

Windows may stick because of temporary swelling in the material of the window or sash in hot or humid conditions. Rubbing paraffin (or wax from an old candle) on the channel may get the window moving easily again. Similarly, a silicone lubricant applied to the tracks of metal-framed windows and sliding-glass doors can help keep them moving freely.

Stains or persistent moisture on interior walls beneath windows may indicate a problem with the window or window well rather than the wall. Have someone direct a wide open spray of water from a hose just along the outside perimeter of the window while you observe the inside. Allow the water to run for at least five minutes. If water leaks around the window, you have found your culprit. If the experiment does not reveal any leaks, look next at problems with condensation, the window well, or a problem with the wall itself.

Reglazing a window in place can be a do-it-yourself project. Follow these steps:

1. Mix oil paint with the glazing compound to create the desired color, or simply plan to paint over the glazing to match the prior color.
2. Remove dried, loose, or cracked glazing compound, dirt, and dust with a clean, dry brush.
3. Replace any missing or damaged *glazier's points* (small metal fasteners that hold the glass in position).
4. Roll a small amount of fresh glazing compound between your hands to stretch it out (the texture is something like modeling clay).
5. Press the compound against the glass and wood with your fingers and smooth it in place with a putty knife. In constant temperatures the compound will gradually dry and harden over a period of about 12 hours.

Broken windowpanes can be replaced by carefully removing the remaining glass, all the old glazing compound and glazier's points, and fitting in an appropriately sized new pane. To replace broken panes framed in materials other than wood, consult the window manufacturer.

Condensation on Windows: Don't panic if condensation forms on your windows during the first spell of cold weather. Your heating system—not your windows—may be the culprit. The humidifier may add too much moisture to the air. The flexible water supply line running from the plumbing lines and connected to the humidifier will lead you to it.

Adjust indoor relative humidity in accordance with outdoor temperatures. When this relationship is out of balance, condensation forms on windows. Check other sources of humidity such as the bathroom. They may need venting to remove excessive humidity.

5

A Seasonal Checklist for Maintaining Your Home

Caring for your home is a year-round commitment, and most tasks can be attended to during any season provided the weather is relatively mild and dry.

The checklist that follows presents a brief summary of major inspection, cleaning, and maintenance tasks associated with different parts of your home. With some variation based on where you live and in what type of house, most of the items in the checklist will apply to your home.

To some extent, the schedule we have recommended is arbitrary. Caring for your home is a year-round commitment, and most tasks can be attended to during any season provided the weather is relatively mild and dry. For certain tasks, however, a specific season is recommended because it is the best time to perform the task. For example, checking for evidence of termites is best done by early to mid-spring, so that termite extermination can take place before the population mushrooms in warmer weather.

Spring and autumn bring their share of storms to most parts of the United States, but they also tend to bring the best weather in much of the country. Early spring and early autumn also are excellent times to check for and correct budding problems related to the extreme temperature changes and storms of the preceding seasons.

Each spring and autumn, check your home's windows, doors, roof, and siding for signs of weather damage. Also check the exterior trim including the soffit and fascia (the areas under the roof overhang) for signs of wear and tear.

Storms and moisture can cause paint to peel, nails to pop, wood to crack or splinter, and vinyl or aluminum siding to come loose.

People who live in parts of the country that enjoy mild summer or winter weather (for all or part of each season) can spread out their exterior repair and maintenance chores over additional weeks or months. And summer and winter can still be excellent seasons for handling interior maintenance tasks. Organizing interior storage, touch-up painting or redecorating (provided you have adequate ventilation and depending on the project), reviewing budgets, and scheduling future appointments for repairs and professional inspections are just a few items that can be well suited to summer or winter.

Whatever schedule you adopt, you will find that establishing a routine for home maintenance is the best way to combat procrastination, manage your maintenance budget, and avoid maintenance overload in any one season.

Like the sections in chapter 4, this checklist has been organized in alphabetical order to make it easy for you to find specific items.

Air Conditioning Systems

Spring □ Check general condition of compressor; remove debris from around compressor as necessary.
□ Check lines to and from compressor.
□ Check motor lubrication.
□ Check, clean blower compartment, fan blades.

Spring and Autumn □ Check air flow, registers, grilles, make sure air flow is unobstructed.

Spring or Autumn □ Schedule professional inspection (annually or biannually).

All Seasons □ Change or clean air filters (monthly to every 3 months during use).

Every 2-4 Years □ Arrange for professional cleaning of complete system, including ductwork.

Appliances

(Ranges, ovens, broilers—controls, thermostats, timers, surfaces, heating elements; pilots and valves; washer and dryer—vents and connections)

Spring and Autumn □ Clear vents of leaves, debris; consider protective cap for vents depending on location and vulnerability to debris, animals.

All Seasons □ Clean gaskets and condenser coils of refrigerators and stand-alone freezers (every 3 months).
□ Follow manufacturers' instructions for routine operation and care of major appliances, including oiling motors.

            ☐ Check, vacuum dryer vents.

Any Season ☐ Schedule annual professional inspection (major appliances, particularly if gas fueled).

Winter ☐ Clear snow, ice away from vents as necessary.

Attics and Attic Crawl Spaces

Any Season ☐ Check insulation coverage of entire ceiling area.

            ☐ Make sure insulation, other material does not block eaves, louvers, attic vents. (If light from the outside shines through vents, then the vents are clear.)

            ☐ Make sure insulation does not directly touch the underside of roof sheathing.

            ☐ Check seals at penetration points.

            ☐ Check unfinished attic for rust spots, rusty nails.

            ☐ Check condition, operation of electrical wiring, switches, outlets.

Winter ☐ Look for frost buildup (sign of excessive moisture.)

Basements

Any Season ☐ Examine interior basement walls and floors for dampness or water stains indicating water seepage, leaks, or poor drainage.

            ☐ Check masonry joints and surfaces.

            ☐ Check flooring for signs of staining, stress cracks.

Bathtubs, Showers, and Lavatories

Any Season ☐ Clean, check surfaces.

            ☐ Check caulking, grout. (Some types of caulking become brittle with age and useless as a water seal. Replace with a long-lasting resilient caulking material, such as silicone or latex.

            ☐ Discourage mildew growth by using bathroom fan to reduce moisture, maintain ventilation.

Carbon Monoxide Detectors

All Seasons ☐ Dust or vacuum to keep dust, debris from interfering with sensors.

            ☐ Test battery and sensor operation monthly; also test hard-wired models after power outages.

            ☐ Reset after testing.

☐ Replace disposable detection cards as directed (usually every few months).

Spring and Autumn ☐ Replace batteries twice a year (battery-powered units).

Carpeting

All Seasons ☐ Vacuum regularly.
☐ Wipe up spills promptly; spot clean stains.
☐ Protect high-traffic areas by rearranging traffic patterns from time to time, and by using area rugs or mats.
☐ Deep clean or steam clean as necessary to remove built-up dirt or stains (however, avoid frequent washing or soaking carpet and padding).

Ceiling Fans

Spring and Autumn ☐ Adjust angle, direction of paddles.

Chimneys and Fireplaces

Spring ☐ Check lining, clean out soot, check for creosote buildup.
☐ Check condition of masonry.

All Seasons ☐ Check condition of chimney cover (cap) and check for birds' nests, obstructions.

Autumn ☐ Schedule professional cleaning and inspection.
☐ Check flue operation.

Any Season ☐ Trim away branches that overhang or come too close to chimney.

Circuit Breakers and Electrical System

Any Season ☐ Check service entrance.
☐ Check outlets, switches, lights.
☐ Check for exposed wires.
☐ Check appliance cords, plugs, and exposed wires for signs of wear.
☐ Label circuits so you know which outlets, devices are served by each circuit.
☐ Calculate amperage required for devices on each circuit.
☐ Call for professional inspection if circuits trip frequently.

☐ Check doorbell, GFCI outlets, exterior (yard) lights for proper operation and check any exposed wiring for signs of wear.

Cleaning

All Seasons   ☐ Routine cleaning and inspection of interior surfaces with deeper cleaning and inspection twice a year (spring and autumn).

Spring, Summer, or Autumn   ☐ General cleaning and inspection of exterior surfaces at least once a year.

All Seasons   ☐ Use compatible cleaning agents; consider use of natural and non-chemical cleaning agents as appropriate.

Crawl Spaces

Spring or Autumn   ☐ Check vapor barrier, insulation, vent(s).

☐ Check condition and placement of vapor barrier if one is in place. (A vapor barrier is usually a polyethylene material that covers 70 to 100 percent of the crawl space, depending on the severity of the moisture problem.)

☐ Check drainage; remove any obstructions.

Decks and Platforms

Spring   ☐ Clean away accumulated debris and dirt.

☐ Check for popped nails, loose screws, bolts.

☐ Check structural supports for signs of insects, rust, moisture damage, digging or chewing by small animals.

☐ Replace weak members.

Spring, Summer, or Autumn   ☐ Refinish with paint, stain, or waterproofing sealants as necessary (every few years).

Doors

(Caulking, sashes, thresholds, hinges, handles, locks, painted surfaces, tracks, rollers, weatherstripping)

Spring and Autumn   ☐ Look for peeling paint, hairline cracks (in wood), dulling finish or scratching on hardware; warping; wear on threshold and weatherstripping.

☐ Examine trim for signs of damage, decay.

☐ Check proper operation of doors, tracks, hinges, locks.

☐ Clean debris and leaves from doorways, thresholds.

☐ Clean weepholes in storm doors.

☐ Repaint in conjunction with exterior trim and siding.

All Seasons ☐ Lubricate moving parts (oil moving parts of garage doors approximately four times a year).

Drains

All Seasons ☐ Check slow drains for clogs; remove hair, grease, other obstructions as necessary.

Winter ☐ Protect exposed and vulnerable pipes against freezing during cold snaps.

Driveways, Walkways, Concrete Steps

Spring ☐ Inspect for cracks, breaks, erosion, cold-weather damage; repair as needed. (If asphalt surfaces need repairing, have the equipment and skills to do a lasting repair job or call a reputable contractor.)

Spring or Autumn ☐ Reseal (optional; reseal only after original seal has worn down significantly).

Winter ☐ Remove wet leaves from paved surfaces.

☐ Remove snow, ice; apply chemical de-icers sparingly, rinse away residue promptly once feasible.

All Seasons ☐ Promptly remove spilled gasoline, oil, turpentine, solvents.

Faucets, Exterior

Autumn or Winter ☐ Drain outside lines and faucets or insulate to protect against freezing.

☐ Disconnect, drain, and store garden hoses.

Fire Extinguishers

Spring and Autumn ☐ Check level of charge once or twice a year; refill or replace as necessary.

Flooring

All Seasons ☐ Clean using products appropriate for the specific flooring materials.

Summer and Winter	☐ Adjust furniture to alter traffic patterns, reduce wear in high-traffic areas.
Any Season	☐ Examine condition of caulking, grout in ceramic tile and laminated plastic floors.
	☐ Repair or replace cracked or discolored tiles.
	☐ Check drainage in basement, foundation floors.
As Needed in Event of Leaks	☐ Pull back floor insulation to check for leaks and wood damage around water supply pipes, drains, water closet.

Foundations

Spring	☐ Check interior foundation walls, floor for signs of moisture, drainage problems.
	☐ Inspect for signs of insect problems; have professional inspect and treat as needed for termites, carpenter ants, powder post beetles, or other pests.
Spring or Autumn	☐ Check for and repair cracks and weakened, crumbling mortar.
Spring and Autumn	☐ Repair concrete (when weather is warm but not hot and relatively dry).
	☐ Clean out clogged weepholes in masonry foundations.
Autumn	☐ Check grading outside foundation.
Autumn and Winter	☐ Clear window wells of leaves and debris.
	☐ Look for signs of excessive condensation.

Furnaces and Heating Systems

(Humidifier, filters, air registers and returns, ducts, dampers, thermostat, blower, burners, motor, pilot, flue or chimney, fuel supply lines)

Spring or Autumn	☐ Check motor lubrication (some systems).
Spring and Autumn	☐ Clean leaves and debris from around an outside condenser (mixed systems) or heat pump unit and trim back shrubs that may block air intake.
	☐ Follow manufacturer's instructions to change unit from summer to winter operation, or from winter to summer operation.
	☐ Test operation of thermostat(s), proper functioning of zoned heating and cooling systems before heating or cooling season begins (or early in season).

Autumn ☐ Schedule a professional cleaning and inspection (annually, biannually, or according to manufacturer's recommendations), including ductwork.
☐ Check fuel supply.

All Seasons ☐ Change air filters monthly or as directed by manufacturer.
☐ Brush or vacuum registers and grilles to keep free of dust, dirt, grime.

Garden

Spring ☐ Check framework of raised garden beds for signs of wear, rot, insect infestation.
☐ Prepare annual beds.

Spring and Summer ☐ Begin seasonal plantings, continuing throughout season.
☐ Fertilize and water regularly.

Spring and Autumn ☐ Plant bulbs, mulch.
☐ Check grading in beds, ensure proper slope so water drains properly away from foundation.

Autumn ☐ Clean and repair garden equipment, remove dirt and rust and store in dry area.

Gutters and Downspouts

Spring and Autumn ☐ Look at gutters, downspouts, splashbacks: Are they at the correct angle?
☐ Run water from hose into gutter, check water exit at downspout: Is the water coming through, going away from foundation?
☐ Clean out leaves, debris, blockages as necessary.
☐ Inspect general condition, including paint, color (fading), look for signs of rust, leaks, loosening of hangers and clips.

Winter ☐ Look for formation of ice dams.

Any Season ☐ Check for damage after severe storms.

Lawns

Spring ☐ Prepare soil, seed, and feed.

Spring and Autumn ☐ Check for changes in grade, erosion, settling, and buildup.

Spring, Summer, and Autumn
- [ ] Spread fertilizer.
- [ ] Inspect for insects.
- [ ] Cut frequently (maintain 2- to 4-inch height during peak growing season for optimum health with most lawn varieties).

Paint, Exterior

(Siding and trim, including shutters)

Spring or Autumn
- [ ] Check paint for signs of fading, blistering, peeling, chalking.
- [ ] Look for signs of water damage.
- [ ] Clean exterior at least once a year.
- [ ] Clean, scrape, sand, prime (as needed), caulk, and paint touch-up areas.
- [ ] Evaluate overall condition, need for general repainting every few years.

Paint, Interior

(Walls, ceilings, baseboards, trim)

Any Season
- [ ] Check color for fading; redecorate as desired.
- [ ] Clean walls, using mild solution, as needed (bathrooms, kitchens, washable paint).
- [ ] Clean, scrape, sand, patch or fill holes, prime (as needed), and paint touch-up areas.
- [ ] Evaluate overall condition, need for general repainting every few years.

Plumbing

All Seasons
- [ ] Check flow of water through pipes; use natural or chemical drain cleaners as needed to promote smooth flow.

Any Season
- [ ] Clean fixtures, faucets with appropriate, nonabrasive cleansers; wipe up splashes promptly.
- [ ] Clean aerators in kitchen, bathroom faucets every 3 to 4 months.
- [ ] Replace aging washers to alleviate drips in faucets.
- [ ] Listen for noise in pipes, other trouble signs.
- [ ] Look for leaks at shutoff valves for laundry equipment.

☐ Check traps, cleanouts, joints when trouble occurs; consult with a professional as needed to solve problems.

Roofs

Spring and Autumn

☐ Inspect roof for snow or storm damage (look at ground as well as roof; check condition of eaves, shingles, flashing).

☐ If the roof has wind turbines, check ball bearings. Clear gable vents of birds' nests and other obstructions.

☐ Examine television antenna guy wires and support straps.

Any Season

☐ Inspect lower edges of sheathing for water damage after storms during primary storm seasons.

☐ Inspect general condition, look for curled, damaged, loose, or missing shingles.

☐ Remove heavy snow loads from flat roofs.

Safety and Security

Any Season

☐ Check function, wear on door and window locks.

☐ Periodically check storage areas, backs of closets, basement corners for potential hazards.

☐ Check stairs, steps, ladders for broken or hazardous areas; check handrails for sturdiness, reliability.

☐ Test operation of lights in infrequently used places.

☐ Test alarms and detectors (alarms at least once or twice annually, depending on system; smoke and carbon monoxide detectors monthly).

☐ Check circuits, inspect sensors.

☐ Test primary and backup batteries, replace as necessary.

☐ Check pressure in fire extinguisher.

☐ Check contents of first aid kit, location of escape ladder.

☐ Test operation of window locks, feasibility of emergency escape routes.

Siding

Spring, Summer, or Autumn

☐ Check siding for loose or missing pieces, lifting or warping, and signs of mildew or moisture damage.

☐ Clean vinyl or aluminum siding using a stiff-bristled broom, water, and a mild soap.

☐ Check condition of flashing, caulking where different materials meet if your home has combinations of one or more materials (for example, part brick, part vinyl siding).

Septic System

Spring, Summer, or Autumn

☐ Check level of septic tank; call for professional cleaning when needed (every other year or so).

☐ Examine drainage field (check grading, firmness of soil); consult professional if you find problems.

Smoke Detectors

All Seasons

☐ Dust or vacuum to keep dust, debris from interfering with sensors.

☐ Test battery and sensor operation monthly; also test hard-wired models after power outages.

☐ Reset after testing (depending on model).

☐ Replace batteries twice a year (battery-powered units).

Termite, Insect Treatments

Spring

☐ Schedule inspection and treatment (as needed) by professional exterminator.

☐ Look for signs of insects, damage in places where wood meets ground; cracks in foundation; areas with negative slope near the foundation or where nearby landscaping retains moisture; penetrations in slab foundations.

☐ Look for holes in wood, spongy or "soft" wood, mud tubes, dropped wings in thresholds, doorsills.

Tools

All Seasons

☐ Clean, store tools properly after each use.

☐ Rinse pesticide and herbicide sprayers to prevent clogging, and rinse fertilizer spreaders to prevent corrosion.

Autumn

☐ Drain yard care power equipment of fuel in late fall or early winter and have it professionally serviced per the manufacturer's instructions.

Winter ☐ File rough spots on hoes and shovels, sharpen blades, and apply linseed oil to handles of garden tools.

Trees and Shrubs

Spring ☐ Check growth, proximity to the house (consider root systems as well as canopies).

Spring or Autumn ☐ Trim shrubs and bushes away from foundation walls and windows (1 foot clearance minimum)
☐ Prune, trim, mulch, according to dormant season of species.

Autumn ☐ Plant, move (most trees and shrubs).

Vent Pipe and Roof Jack

Spring ☐ Check for weather-related damage and to ensure free air movement around vents and louvers.
☐ Clean screens, remove birds' nests, spiders, insects, and dust.

Walls and Ceilings, Interior

Any Season ☐ Check for cracks, loose or failing plaster, signs of leaks or stains, dirt, and finish damage.
☐ Check for odor or visible evidence of mildew and mold.
☐ Check for cracks where ceilings join walls and where moldings attach to ceilings and walls.
☐ Check for fading of paint color (see Painting, Interior).
☐ Reset popped nails, fill nail holes, patch small cracks or abrasions in wallboard.

Water Heater

All Seasons ☐ Check temperature setting (lowering temperature setting can sometimes alleviate noise in pipes).
☐ Check operation of pressure relief valve every 3 to 4 months.
☐ Look for signs of leaks or rusting, particularly at bottom of tank or at pipe connections.
☐ Drain a small amount of water once or twice a year to eliminate mineral deposits and debris that may have settled at bottom of tank.

Windows

Spring and Autumn ☐ Check window locks, glass, screens.
☐ Clean glass and screens regularly.
☐ Check weatherstripping for damage and tightness of fit.
☐ Clean debris and leaves from below-grade window wells and storm drains.
☐ Clean weepholes on all sliders.
☐ Examine trim for signs of damage or decay.
☐ Check condition of glazing compounds and caulking.

Any Season ☐ Check for evidence of moisture between pane and storm windows.
☐ Check window operation; examine all hardware and lubricate moving parts.

Quick Lists

Creating a notebook of summary information for quick reference may be the simplest way to collect and track information about your home maintenance activities. The form that follows includes space for recording important purchase and warranty information. Photocopy and fill in the forms as you get to various tasks. Placed in a notebook, these quick lists will provide an easily updatable record of your activities.

Date: _____

Quick List: _____

(Fill in name of item or task.)

Purchase

☐ Item _____

☐ Closing Date (if Conveyed with House)

_____

☐ Purchase Date (if Replaced or Added)

_____

☐ Purchased From _____

☐ Model No. _____

☐ Serial No. _____

Owner's Manual/Instructions

☐ Received with Item

☐ Filed with Important Papers

Warranty

☐ Item(s) Under Warranty

☐ Warranty Number _____

☐ Warranty Terms or Conditions Reviewed

☐ Date Warranty Period Begins _____

☐ Date Warranty Expires _____

☐ Warranty Contact Name and Telephone

Number _____

_____

Insurance

☐ Documented for Homeowners' Insurance

☐ Policy Number _____

☐ Replacement Value _____

☐ Insurance Contact Name and Telephone

Number _____

_____

Routine Cleaning

☐ Daily ☐ Weekly ☐ Monthly

☐ Semiannually ☐ Annually

☐ Manufacturer's Instructions:

_____

Professional Cleaning and Inspection

☐ Annually (Semiannually

☐ As Needed for Major Repair/Replacement

Homeowner's Maintenance Check

_____

_____

_____

_____

_____

_____

_____

_____

_____

_____

Notes or Special Instructions

_____

_____

_____

_____

_____

_____

_____

_____

6

The Homeowner's Toolkit

Having the appropriate tools on hand makes caring for your home much easier. It is not necessary, however, to purchase a large number of specialty tools. A fairly short list of tools and supplies will keep you going in most situations, and the more specialized equipment needed for occasional tasks often can be rented for a nominal amount. This chapter offers a basic list of tools every homeowner should keep handy, and provides additional information on some of the listed items to help you get the most from your tools. Some attention is paid to tools associated with painting as this is a relatively frequent task faced by most homeowners.

Having the appropriate tools on hand makes caring for your home much easier.

Tools and Supplies

A good start-up toolbox will include the following items:

- adjustable wrench
- assorted nails, brads, screws, nuts, bolts, and washers
- assorted rags
- buckets
- caulking gun
- claw hammer
- duplicate keys
- fire extinguisher
- first aid kit

- hand saw
- leaf rake
- level
- needle-nose pliers with wirecutter
- plane
- putty knife
- rubber mallet
- safety goggles
- screwdrivers (small, medium, and large with standard and Phillips heads)
- small electric drill
- standard hand pliers
- tape measure
- work gloves

Most of the items in this list will fit in a mid-sized toolbox or chest easily storable in a closet or on a garage shelf. Additional items to acquire as needed include:

- A-frame step ladder
- additional power tools, such as a circular saw or power sander
- bungee cords, nylon cord, or rope at various lengths
- edger
- electric screwdriver
- extension ladder
- lawn mower
- mortar board
- paint brushes (4-inch wall, 2-inch trim, and angled 2-inch sash or trim brushes)
- paint rollers, handles, and extension rod
- reusable paint pans and pan liners
- roof rake
- sanding board
- shovel(s)
- snow blower
- staple gun
- tarp(s)
- trowel, joint trowel
- weed-whacker
- wheel barrow or garden cart

Brushes

Paintbrushes range in price from less than $4 to more than $60. Natural-bristle brushes are considered the best quality brush. A good quality natural bristle or synthetic bristle brush will last for years. Recommended uses are usually listed on the brush package, and the bristle type often is stamped on the handle of each brush for easy identification. Regardless of price, some brushes are well made and others are not. Look at the tips of the bristles. A well-made natural bristle brush has little flags on the ends; good synthetic brushes have fuzzy-looking tips. Give the bristles a hard rap against the counter. All brushes will lose some bristles, but the poorly made ones will lose more. Check the metal band around the brush handle. Usually made of aluminum or stainless steel, the band should be tightly wrapped and secured all around the brush.

Use only natural-bristle brushes or top-quality synthetic-bristle brushes with oil-based paints. Natural-bristle brushes are ideal for carrying a full charge of the heavier oil-based paints. Polyester or nylon brushes provide the best results when used with latex semi-gloss or flat paint.

Inexpensive disposable brushes save cleanup time at the end of the job; however, you always want a brush that will be sturdy enough not to disintegrate during painting.

Keep several different size brushes on hand. A 4-inch brush can cut down the amount of time spent covering exterior siding. A 1- or 2-inch brush is useful for painting trim, ornamental designs, or hard-to-reach areas such as behind downspouts or gutters. Brushes are typically available from 1/8-inch or 1/4-inch in width up to 8 inches or larger. Angled brushes make it easier to cover door or window sashes without getting paint on the glass. The professionals at your local home center or paint supply store can assist you in selecting the right brushes for the job.

Of course, painting involves a variety of other tools, such as edger pads and rollers, paint pans and liners, various styles of scrapers, and sanding tools, some of which appear in Figure 27. Most tools are available in a variety of sizes and shapes.

Paint Rollers

Paint rollers are wonderful time- and labor-saving applicators. Rollers and related paint applicators (pads, wheels, and so forth) cost anywhere from $2 to $20. Rollers also come in different widths, generally from 2 inches to a standard 9 inches. Rollers designed for use on flat surfaces can be found as large as 18 inches wide. Smaller rollers are convenient for more confined areas such as trim boards, while larger rollers make quick work of expansive stretches of wall, ceiling, or siding.

A roller is actually made up of two pieces—the handle and the cover. The handle includes the grip and the frame onto which the cover is secured. The frame can be either a birdcage style or solid metal. Birdcage roller frames work best with fast-drying paints because they clean up more easily than the solid-metal frames. The birdcage style also weighs less.

Roller covers are available in different nap sizes and fabrics. The nap size is the length of the material on the roller cover. Choose longer naps for rough surfaces, short ones for smooth finishes. For most jobs a nap of 1/4 inch to 3/8

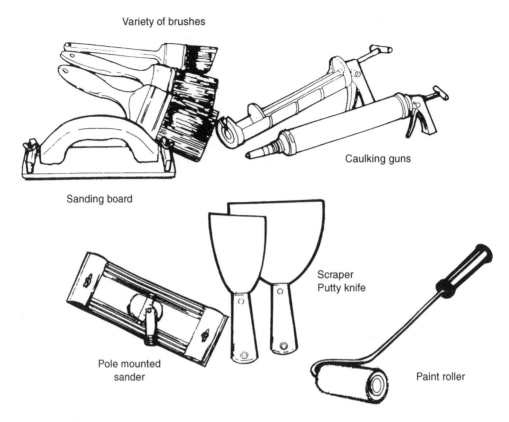

Variety of brushes

Sanding board

Caulking guns

Scraper
Putty knife

Pole mounted
sander

Paint roller

FIGURE 27 An assortment of frequently used painting tools.

inch will provide a clean, smooth surface. Under the nap is either a cardboard or plastic sleeve. Plastic sleeves are best suited for water-thinned paints; cardboard sleeves work best with solvent-thinned paints.

Roller covers are made from natural or synthetic fibers. As with brushes, the natural rollers are best used with oil (alkyd) products while the synthetic covers work best with latex products. Roller covers usually are labeled with their intended use.

Be sure to purchase compatible handles and roller covers. Not all covers fit all handles. Also, don't skimp on roller covers: you'll save yourself time and frustration by buying all the covers you'll need up front.

Specialty rollers designed for painting trim work come in many shapes and sizes. A useful roller accessory is an extension handle. Most roller handles have a threaded hole at the base to accommodate the insertion of a threaded wood or metal pole. An extension handle allows you to reach farther without using or moving your ladder.

Scrapers and Sanders

Whatever style scraper you use, keep in mind the following points:

- Handle the scraper blade carefully to prevent possible injury.
- Hold the scraper at no more than a 45° angle while applying only moderate pressure; a more radical angle or heavier pressure increases the risk that you will slip and injure yourself or gouge the wood.
- Move the scraper along the surface in smooth, controlled strokes for the best results.
- Stop scraping when the surface is fairly smooth. You need not remove all the old paint down to bare wood; your goal is simply to even out the surface and remove flaking or peeling paint that might crumble when the new paint is applied.

Sanding is possibly the most dreaded part of any refinishing job, but it is absolutely essential. Two different grits of sandpaper should handle most jobs. A medium grit (number 50) sandpaper will quickly remove layers of paint from a wood surface. Follow this with a fine grit (number 120) sandpaper to smooth the surface and feather out any ragged edges.

Sanding by hand goes easier when you wrap the sandpaper around a block of wood. Sanding by hand is recommended for delicate wood trim or other areas where you don't want to risk accidentally wearing away too much of the surface. Using a hand-held, electric orbital sander for broad, flat areas of siding will save you considerable time. Be sure to keep the sander moving at all times to prevent sanding away or burning the wood surface. Orbital sanders are relatively inexpensive and come in handy for many home projects.

You also can purchase accessories to convert a power drill into a sander. A disk pad attachment fits directly into your drill's chuck and provides a platform for sanding disks. Use both medium and fine grit disks to ensure a properly prepared painting surface. Barrel sander attachments also are available. The barrel sander is especially useful for cleaning up areas such as trim work and the undersides of clapboards.

For sanding in corners, an electric triangle sander is a real timesaver. The triangle-shaped head of this power sander allows it to fit into corners and along joints.

If you have not used a power sander before it's a good idea to practice on a piece of scrap lumber before you start in on your house. Keep the following tips in mind:

- Get the feel of the drill as you hold it at different angles. Going around edges and under overhangs will require you to hold the drill many different positions.
- Apply only slight pressure. Layers of paint are relatively thin. It's easy to apply too much pressure, and you can quickly strip away large amounts of wood.
- Let the sandpaper and the drill do the work. The drill is turning at approximately 2,500 revolutions per minute; a light touch not only saves the wood, it also helps the disk glide along the surface.

Ladders

Ladders come in many different varieties, some of which are shown in Figure 28. Buying a ladder is no place to skimp on quality. Most ladders are made of aluminum, wood, or fiberglass, and come in four basic grades: light household duty; commercial (for painters and general repair); industrial (for contractors and full-time service people); and professional (for heavy-duty industrial and construction use). Many professionals prefer only top-quality, industrial-grade aluminum ladders.

When you shop for a ladder, look on the side rails for a label listing its grade and rated weight capacity. The following ratings are common:

- type III (household grade), usually rated at 200 pounds
- type II (commercial grade), usually rated at 225 pounds
- type I (industrial grade), usually rated at 250 pounds
- professional grade, usually rated at 300 pounds

Most homeowners purchase a common A-frame ladder at some point. This type of ladder has hinged supports that allow it to fold up for easier stor-

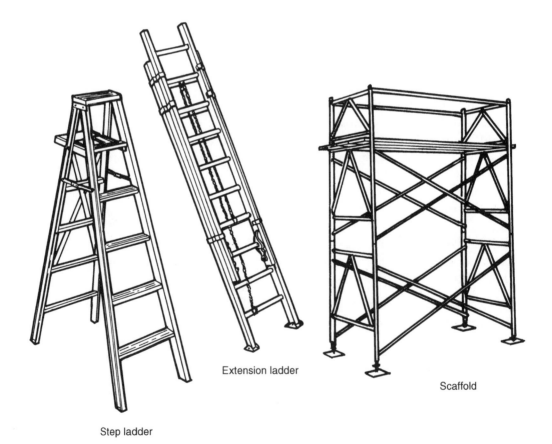

Extension ladder

Scaffold

Step ladder

FIGURE 28 Typical ladders and scaffolding used when painting.

age and carrying. The hinges must be fully extended and locked down when the ladder is in use; they are the main supports keeping the ladder in place.

When using an A-frame ladder place all four legs on a solid, level surface. The taller a ladder is, the more unstable it becomes. A person's weight on one side of the ladder adds to that instability. When working on a ladder keep your body weight balanced over the center part of ladder's rungs, or steps. Do not stretch or overreach while on a ladder—this causes a shift in weight and can easily pull the ladder off balance. Also do not climb to the topmost rung or stand on the top of the ladder. At the top of the ladder the slightest shift in weight can cause the ladder to topple over. Most ladders today include a notice indicating how far up you can safely climb.

The most useful ladder for a homeowner to own may be the aluminum extension ladder. Extension ladders provide more support at greater heights. These ladders use locking mechanisms to secure an adjustable top section to a stable bottom section. A well-made 20-foot aluminum extension ladder costs about $350. Professional versions can cost considerably more.

Before climbing an extension ladder always make sure the locking hooks are securely fastened to the rungs of the bottom portion and that the ladder has been placed on firm, level ground. To test the ladder for stability, climb up a rung or two and, with both feet parallel to the ground, jiggle in place. No rocking motion should be detectable. The feet of the ladder may be fitted with metal or plastic shoes that have teeth to grip the ground and help keep the ladder stable.

Usually the upper part of the ladder will rest against the side of the house. To place an extension ladder at a safe angle, think of the ladder as the longest leg in a triangle formed with the house. For every 4 feet of height compensate with 1 foot of width at the base. For example, if the ladder will be extended approximately 16 feet, for proper support the base of the ladder should be 4 feet out from the wall (see also Safety in chapter 4).

Scaffolding

When properly set up and placed on solid footing, scaffolding provides an exceptionally sound platform to work from. The downside is threefold: it's difficult to set up without at least two people; it can be quite expensive; and it requires considerable storage space. Most homeowners will rent rather than purchase scaffolding.

Safety checks are a necessity before each use. Check screw legs, brackets, trusses, and braces for proper fit and any signs of damage before you climb up. Damaged or ill-fitting components must be replaced. Scaffolding also requires a solid, level surface for the base footings. Do not place scaffolding on an unstable footing such as loose bricks, rocks, or boxes.

Snowblowers

Early snowblowers suffered a reputation for being awkward, uncooperative, hard-to-start, enormous contraptions. Today snowblowers are available in many sizes, shapes, and configurations. The two types of snowblowers most used by homeowners fall between the two extremes of size (see Figure 29). In locales that experience very wet and heavy snowfalls, heavy-duty four-cycle machines offer greater horsepower and a two-stage auger and impeller system. Lighter, fluffier snowfalls can be adequately managed by single-stage, two-cycle snowblowers. Two-cycle machines are available with engines of various degrees of horsepower. A good rule of thumb when buying a snowblower is to buy slightly more than you need. For example, if the average snowfall in your area is 3 to 6 inches at a time and the snow is normally powdery, a 4 or 5 horsepower engine will probably be sufficient. By moving up to a 6 or 7 horsepower engine you will be prepared for the occasional blizzard.

Like your lawnmower, your snowblower should receive an annual check-up by a qualified technician. Routinely changing worn drive belts, tightening loose bolts, lubricating drive shafts, and replacing worn or missing shear pins will help prevent your snowblower from quitting in the middle of a snowstorm.

Renting Equipment

Items a homeowner might consider renting to make various maintenance jobs easier include power-sprayers, high-pressure washers, pneumatic nail or staple guns, scaffolding, roof hoists, or conveyor belts. Renting tools makes sense as long as you know how to safely use the items.

Enjoying your house and property to the fullest without unnecessary major expenses means caring for your investment like a member of the family. This book has provided a blueprint for organizing the many areas of home maintenance into logical and manageable segments. Once adapted to your specific lifestyle and location, this blueprint can be a valuable help as you care for your home for many years to come.

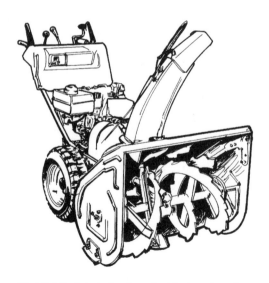

FIGURE 29 Left: A typical heavy-duty four-cycle snow blower. Right: A typical medium-duty two-cycle snow blower. Both are powered by gasoline engines.

Additional Books for Consumers from BuilderBooks

Building Your Home: An Insider's Guide

Building a home...the experience is complicated, exciting, scary, fun, expensive, gratifying, time-consuming, and wonderful—sometimes all in the same day. With this book, you learn firsthand about the home building process and dealing with builders from an experienced industry professional. Author Carol Smith is a leading customer relations consultant for the home building industry with 21 years of experience in such positions as vice president of customer relations, orientation rep, construction superintendent, real estate broker, property manager, and mortgage lender. *Building Your Home: An Insider's Guide* takes you step-by-step through the home building process and helps you find a comfortable balance among quality, features, and price.

"If you are planning to build or buy a new home, read this book now . . . or wish you had later."

Sam Bradley, *Builder, Sam Bradley Homes, Springfield, Missouri*

"I wish I had read this book before I remodeled my home!"

Betty James, *Homeowner, Silver Spring, Maryland*